Sex in Silicon Valley

Sex in Silicon Valley

the geeks in the Valley are getting more than you'd think

Kiana Tower

Writers Club Press
San Jose New York Lincoln Shanghai

Sex in Silicon Valley
the geeks in the Valley are getting more than you'd think

Writers Club Press
an imprint of iUniverse, Inc.

For information address:
iUniverse, Inc.
5220 S. 16th St., Suite 200
Lincoln, NE 68512
www.iuniverse.com

ISBN: 0-595-20848-7

Printed in the United States of America

for our friends and colleagues
and all the people who make working,
living and dating in Silicon Valley an adventure

Contents

Acknowledgements

This book would not have been possible without the more than 300 Bay Area residents who freely gave us their time, their feedback and most importantly, their true stories about Sex in Silicon Valley.

Thank you.

Introduction

Imagine this...

You're out with friends somewhere in the Bay Area. The wine and banter are flowing freely. As you drink and laugh, the conversation turns to sex. Everyone has a story to tell, and the more stories people tell, the more the laughter flows.

"Okay, Okay...what's the most unusual place you've ever had sex?" you ask your friends. "Your ideal sexual encounter? Your worst dating disaster?" All sorts of funny and memorable stories come up. This book is about those stories.

Some come on in, pull up a chair, have a drink, and read on...

A Word About Silicon Valley

Statistics show Bay Area denizens read more books, have more years of schooling, and as we go to press, have the highest per capita income in the nation. This affluent, literate, highly educated populace seems to have everything going for it. Up until the recent dot com bust, tales of newly minted millionaires and optionaires paying cash for houses and cars dominated the media. Silicon Valley was the place where financial dreams came true for anyone smart enough or lucky enough to hit a pot of stock option gold.

But along with the reputation for free-flowing wealth came a stereotype of the Silicon Valley geek leading a terribly dull life. Endless hours in a cubicle. No social life. And certainly no sex.

This book, written during the tail end of the dot com boom and the beginning of the dot com bust, may just shatter that geek stereotype. While admittedly those of us who live here in the Valley do work insane hours in cube farms, we do have social lives, and we do have sex.

Sex in Silicon Valley combines stories and research from more than 300 Silicon Valley residents, ranging in age from 21 to 56, from graphic designers to rocket scientists. This book is about those great stories of what we're really doing here when we're not ensconced in our cubicles. Or when we are in our cubicles…and no one else is around.

Researching Sex in Silicon Valley

But more than just great stories, the authors were interested in gathering statistical data on the Silicon Valley dating scene. (Hey, what kind of geeks would we be if we didn't gather data?) The dating scene here fascinated us, and not just because we live and date here ourselves. Silicon Valley is filled with such a diverse population of people, an extraordinarily bright collection of tech-oriented folks from every corner of the globe. Even in today's tough economic times, the Valley is still instilled with a spirit of innovation—the feeling that with enough hard work and combined brain power, anything is possible. This is a fascinating place to live and work.

We designed an extensive web survey, polling Silicon Valley and Bay Area residents about dating, relationships and their social lives. We got the word out using popular bulletin boards, such as craigslist (www.craigslist.org). Within hours of its launch, our survey site had attracted more than a thousand hits!

In addition, we conducted in-person interviews with colleagues, friends and everyone we knew, with a promise of complete anonymity. Over various dinners of margaritas, sushi and pizza, we continued to ask questions and gather data. After months of research, we had more than 300 usable surveys and first-person interviews. Our research was complete. And, to our delight, we discovered there truly is Sex in Silicon Valley!

But…how do you define Silicon Valley?

Who knows? Silicon Valley is a state of mind, rather than a physical state. The term 'Silicon Valley' originally appeared in a 1971 article in the

Electronic News, but legend has it the name was actually coined in a topless bar in Palo Alto and originally referred to a *silicone* valley. From the beginning, sex and Silicon Valley have been inescapably linked.

Some folks say Silicon Valley stretches all the way up to Marin County and all the way down to the sleepy towns around Santa Cruz. On the other hand, some San Franciscans wouldn't be caught dead being considered part of Silicon Valley, as they consider themselves much too hip to be lumped in with all those engineers, programmers and scientists.

We invited our survey respondents to choose whatever definition worked for them. As long as they lived somewhere in the Bay Area, we were content to consider them as part of the mysterious, ever-expanding place known as "Silicon Valley." Many residents of this area use the terms "Silicon Valley" and "the Bay Area" interchangeably, as will we throughout the book. We could just as easily have called this book *Sex in the Bay Area*, but the title didn't seem nearly as catchy.

What You are About to Read

Some of our survey respondents provided a great deal of detail in telling their stories, so we have included their tales here with little editing, other than grammatical and punctuation corrections.

Other survey respondents provided wonderful tidbits, but with little narrative to tie their stories together cohesively. In these cases, we judiciously added enough narrative to help story flow. We were careful not to change the context or intent of any of the stories. All of the actual events, moods and feelings remain completely true to the original survey responses.

But enough about how we conducted the research for this book. Let's get on to the stories.

The geeks of Silicon Valley are getting a lot more than you'd think!

Chapter One

Unique and Interesting Sex (and other fun things)

Silicon Valley and the Bay Area attract people of all types, from all over the world. Most of the transplants who settle here have something in common: a spirit of adventure. Those who buy into the stereotype of a cubicle-bound engineer would scoff at the thought of such a person having a spirit of adventure.

But to uproot yourself from familiar surroundings and transplant yourself thousands of miles away where the only person you know is your landlord, takes courage of a special kind. These folks—the engineers, sales and marketing folks, web artists and designers—are people of a unique and interesting sort.

Our survey tapped into their spirit of adventure with questions like, "What's the most unusual place you've ever had sex?" and "Describe the best sexual encounter you've ever had." Our respondents allowed us to peek into their intimate lives and demonstrated just how unique and interesting Valley denizens are. Here are their stories.

*   *   *

Lucky

Lucky is 32, single and lives in San Francisco. His most unusual encounter occurred in the basement of a dive bar: "We were walking home after cocktails and could not wait to tear into each other. We kept rolling around in doorways and on hoods of cars and grinding up against buildings all the way back to her apartment. At one point we actually fell over and did not stop making out, right on the sidewalk. Finally, we just couldn't wait any longer and ran into some Chinese dive bar in the Tenderloin. We went downstairs and screwed our brains out 'til the bar owner came and almost knocked the door down, yelling he would call the cops unless we stopped…at least I think that's what he said since it was all in Chinese."

Laurie

Laurie is a 25 year-old consultant, originally from New York. While Laurie describes the people in the Bay Area as "not as friendly and approachable" as back east, she is not having any problems with the dating scene. Laurie describes her single status as "single and swinging." She's had seven dates in the past month, and has had sex more than 10 times. When asked to rate the quality of sexual partners out here in the Bay Area, Laurie admits that sex is better than in her native New York. "People like to spice it up out here more," says Laurie.

Laurie's most unusual sexual encounter happened doggy-style at PacBell Park near the statue of Willie Mays. Laurie didn't provide too many details about time of day, or how the encounter came about, but she describes her experience as follows: "It was on the statue in front of PacBell Park. Doggy-style, getting thrusted into, while holding on to the statue of 'Willie' for dear life."

Doug

For those who had a story to tell, but didn't wish to fill out the survey, SexinSiliconValley.com offered a free-form "submit your story" form. Doug used the form to email us the following interesting tidbit:

"The most interesting thing that happened to me recently was getting drunk with a beautiful lesbian friend. She had been fantasizing about screwing a man using a strap-on dildo.

Even though I had never done anything like that, I was so taken with her that I let her do whatever she wanted. I'm glad I took the risk. We ended up dating almost a year! For those of you curious about the dildo, it didn't hurt at all, much to my surprise. I'd describe it as fun, although not necessarily sexually exciting. We did find all manner of other interesting things to do during the year we were dating...

With regards to my getting laid in the Bay Area, I think it's really hard unless you are an attractive, stylish extrovert, or you have good friends that sleep with you. I usually go the latter route, but I think I'm running out of friends to sleep with.

I've replied to a number of "women seeking men" ads (online) but have barely gotten a response. It's tough competing with a large number of responses from other guys...at least, that's what I tell myself!

I'm 34 and it seems like most women my age are already married or engaged. I don't want to date much younger women, and it's hard to find older women that I'm attracted to.

So, I guess the key is to keep working on yourself, and be confident.

And, don't let those hideous craigslist blind dates smash your self-esteem!"

Todd

Todd left his native San Diego a few years ago, coming to the Bay Area to be with his then girlfriend. In his early 30s, he is a national account manager in San Francisco and is divorced. Here, Todd recounts one of his most unusual adventures:

"My brother came over with some friends, and one of them was this little hottie. We hit it off instantly. Wanting to be alone to talk, we left our friends and headed out into the cold weather. After a while, we ended up in a Laundromat to avoid the cold weather outside," Todd recalls. As it turned out, the Laundromat got a little more action than spinning and rinsing that night.

"Before we knew it, we were on the floor in the back of the Laundromat having sex," he says. Just when things were about to reach a climax, they heard someone enter the Laundromat. They scrambled for their clothes, making quite a racket. But by the time they peeked out, no one was there. The couple parted, and Todd headed home.

Later, his brother told him a woman had come out of the Laundromat in a panic. She was telling people not to go into the Laundromat because she had heard noises and thought someone was hiding in the back waiting to attack her.

Randy

Randy, male, age 29, moved to Silicon Valley from Oregon for "fame, fortune, and the cheese." He's enjoyed both cybersex and face-to-face encounters with people he's met online.

The most unusual place Randy's had sex is "behind the cash register at a record store. I worked there at the time, and it was open for business! It was so much fun knowing we could have been caught at anytime! Imagine someone walking up to the register to ask for the latest Kenny G and finding me back there screwing someone's brains out."

Don

Don, 28, describes an intriguing rendezvous at the Sacramento County Fair:

"Last year, I was walking through the fairgrounds with my girlfriend, and our hormones go the better of us. We'd spent the whole day enjoying the games and events. We saw a booth that had been cleared out for the day and sneaked behind it for some one-on-one action. Since it was going to be a quickie, we did it doggy-style, with her bent over on the table. Since the booth was pretty far off from the others, she was yelling and screaming as though no one could hear us. This totally aroused me, and I pulled out and came on the ground. We walked out with big grins on our faces!"

Silicon Valley is notorious for the long hours worked by its many high-tech inhabitants. It's only natural then that the needs of the flesh sometimes get combined with the convenience of the workplace.

Jack

Jack is a 28 year-old male, born and raised in California. Jack has worked in San Diego, Fresno and the UK, but most of his career experience has been centered around Silicon Valley. Jack's led a colorful career, starting out as a bike messenger in downtown San Francisco. He holds degrees in medicine and business administration, but comments "neither of my degrees is relevant to my current position."

Jack recently told us about his experiences in the Valley. "I'd been working for this Silicon Valley company for approximately three years. The first year was the usual—new to the company, no frills stuff—and it went by rather slowly."

Things became more interesting with the arrival of a new co-worker. "One day I spotted a new admin assistant, Judi, down the hall from where I work. Her long blonde hair was more than I could handle, and I kept saying to myself 'only in your dreams.' It was not too long after she started that she began flirting with me. We started spending lunch together just chatting about superficial stuff."

After almost a year of being friends, Jack and Judi became closer. "She started opening up more about her ever unfulfilled libido, and it changed the way I saw her. She was no longer a friend but this girl who had needs to be fulfilled. I could see her boyfriend was just not taking care of business as he should have been," says Jack.

One day Judi invited Jack to her apartment for lunch. "I thought about it, and I guess I was hoping something would happen. But I would not have been disappointed had it not," he says. After lunch, Judi indulged in a little "smoking therapy" while Jack abstained.

"After a few minutes she started coming on to me, and we had sex on her sofa in the living room where she and her boyfriend would watch TV. I was a little concerned but lost that rather quickly. The sex was incredible, she was clean shaven and perfect in every way. From her breasts to her inner thighs. I ravished her body for a good half an hour or so," recalls Jack.

Fulfilled, they decided to head back to the office to finish off the rest of the day. Later in the day Judi showed Jack the damage from the lunchtime rendezvous—skinned knees and a few bruises from tumbling around on the sofa.

Their relationship continued on and off for a good year, and they still work together today. "On occasion, we make plans to meet for an evening of fun; that always makes for a less than productive workweek afterwards. The sex is excellent and the fact that we do not have to have a relationship to have this makes it all the more alluring. We usually meet at hotels around the Peninsula or down in the South Bay," confides Jack.

"Sex definitely makes going to work easier. You can make a dollar and at the same time have fun doing it. In a high-stress work environment, we all need a little release. I feel that the excitement of having sex with co-workers makes up for the lack of excitement in other parts of my life!"

Currently, Jack is involved with a second co-worker. "Sex with co-workers is a lot easier than most people imagine," concludes Jack. "I highly recommend it."

Betty

Betty's best sexual encounter ever occurred with a co-worker. She came out to the Bay Area a year ago for a job opportunity, and found more opportunities than just career advancement.

"The opportunity to physically connect with this co-worker came in a most unlikely place—on the floor of an office in the history building at Stanford University," says Betty. "It was an extremely meditative experience. We were so connected, mentally. As we slid in and out of each other, my entire body felt alive, packed with nerve endings. That was the good part. The bad part was that we were in an uncomfortable and shabby place. I was lying on my back as he pumped into me, and the carpet was very scratchy against my skin, distracting me from some of the pleasure of what was happening. And, once, the janitor came by the door, which temporarily interrupted the flow of what we were doing."

When asked what her ideal sexual experience would be, Betty says: "with someone I totally trust, who understands me, and in a place where there are no scratchy carpets or intrusive janitors."

Tammy

Tammy is a 26 year-old counselor, who was born and raised in Silicon Valley. Tammy is currently in a relationship and enjoying the sexual aspects of being involved with someone. "I'd rank our last sexual encounter as an eight. Since we have a good relationship, it wasn't just sex. It was making love, which is much more passionate than just having sex to fulfill a physical urge."

Tammy's most unusual sexual encounter happened with a previous boyfriend. "This guy I was dating worked swing shift at a computer company. I stopped by to see him, and we were both feeling rather…uh, amorous," says Tammy. "We went into the conference room, closed the door, and started having sex on the table. That turned out to be rather awkward, so we ended up finishing it on the floor instead. There's something to be said for having sex in an unusual, forbidden, place."

Chapter Two

Sex, Cybersex and the Internet

Silicon Valley is known for its entrepreneurial spirit. Many of our survey respondents have applied this same enterprising thinking to their dating lives to meet the challenges of dating in the Valley.

Not surprisingly, the Internet is the communications tool of choice for Bay Area singles. The most popular hangouts include craigslist (www.craigslist.org) and Yahoo! Chat. The majority of our survey respondents have experienced online romance; 55 percent of men and 56 percent of women have tried cybersex. Even more—61 percent of men and 38 percent of women—have used the Internet to generate face-to-face meetings and sexual encounters.

The results? Definitely a mixed bag. Some respondents are enjoying fascinating sexual encounters they would not have otherwise. Others have experienced their worst dating disasters after setting up a face-to-face meeting with someone they met online. And most fall somewhere in between.

Here are true stories of sex, cybersex, and online dating in the Bay Area.

*   *   *

Nicole

Nicole is 30, a marketing consultant and a native of Silicon Valley. She submitted this story in its entirety. She calls it *The Craigslist Chronicles*.

"Last year, I was working for a start-up, now a soon to be defunct new-media venture. I was working 14-hour days and most weekends, leaving little time for dating or a relationship. In fact, several of my co-workers ended relationships they were in because of the workload and stress.

One night, I was chatting with a friend, lamenting my man-less status and telling her I didn't think I would ever have time to meet someone, let alone develop a relationship. The stress and lack of sex were taking their toll, and I was on edge.

She said, 'Nic, why don't you just have a fling?'

'A what?'

'A fling. A one-night stand. A fuck. Just go out and get laid!'

Honestly, it had never occurred to me. I thought, 'That's so not me.' But with my friend's encouragement, I thought I'd give it a shot.

But where would I find someone to fling me? I'm not a bar-type, and wouldn't even consider sex with a coworker. I ended up on craigslist, a local community web site. I'd found my job and my apartment on craigslist, so why not a flinger?

I posted an ad in the 'Casual Encounters' section of the personals and received hundreds of responses. They were coming in literally faster than I could read them. So I stopped reading them. I decided to answer an ad instead. It just seemed easier.

I found one I liked and wrote to him. He answered within minutes. He was a chef, which I thought was very cool. He sounded good and his picture was pretty cute, so we set up a meeting for later that week.

When we met, I was so nervous my hands were shaking! We went to a hotel, and, well, I hope he is better in the kitchen than in the bedroom! The sex was not spectacular. It was barely passable. He told me to call if I wanted to get together again, but I'd already decided against it.

On the way home, I was struck by this amazing feeling of freedom. I realized I never had to see this guy again. Never would wonder if he was going to call. If I wanted to see him, I would call (I didn't and wouldn't). It was completely in my control. The feeling was fabulous.

Men are so lucky. They know about this already. Why haven't they clued us in? Women buy into the Cinderella, fairy tale crap and think that sex and love are inexorably linked. Wrong!

Even though my first 'casual encounter' was less than stellar, I decided to try it again. I posted another ad, specifying what I wanted. And again, the responses poured in. I chose a few and wrote back, then selected the next candidate.

My second encounter was much better. He was a military recruiter. Very clean cut, which I love. Tall, lean and so, so polite. We met at a motel and talked for about an hour before actually doing the deed. He was sweet and adequate, but not someone I wanted to see again. I enjoyed talking to him more than screwing him; he was an interesting guy. Just as before, the feeling of freedom afterward was better than the actual sex. I was amazed at how easy it was. Most people who know me would say I was far too conservative to do something like this.

I decided I'd try it once more, and if that didn't work out, I'd quit. I arranged a meeting for the following week with an investment banker from San Francisco. I was a little worried since he refused to send a picture, but I knew I could just walk away if I wasn't attracted to him, or vice-versa. We met at the train station in downtown San Jose, since he was coming down from the City. He turned out to be a total hottie. Tall, clean-cut and wickedly cute. I guess he liked what he saw, too.

We made our way to a motel (even with my newfound brazenness, I would never bring someone home, or go to a stranger's home), where we walked around the block and talked for a while, then decided to go to the room and get busy. We kissed, and he kissed just how I like a man to kiss—not too soft, not too firm. He was dee-lish! I could have kissed him for hours, but I knew anyone that could kiss like that would have other talents.

He stripped quickly, but was very attentive to me as I undressed, caressing me and helping me disrobe. We moved to the bed and he knelt between my legs and put those amazing lips to work down there. Now, I am not like most women. I actually prefer penetration to oral. I mean, oral is okay, but I really, really love feeling a man inside me. Nothing else comes close.

I begged him to put it in me, and as he stood up, I got my first good look at his equipment. He was quite well endowed. But it was curved! I had never seen a curved penis before. I tried not to stare, but really, how could I not? I guess he was pretty sensitive about it because he'd steered me away from it thus far.

I wondered if it would hurt. Or if it hurt him. I mean, does it straighten out inside???

He lowered himself into me, and OH MY GOD!

It was fabulous! We went at it for good, long time, then he flipped me over and entered me from behind. I'd heard about g-spots, but had never experienced that particular delight until that moment. I couldn't stop moaning. All I can say is a curved penis is the best!

While the experience was great, I have given up online dating, and my craigslist days are over. After my company went bust, I had plenty of time to get out and meet someone…and ended up dating a former co-worker I'd been eyeing. He doesn't have a curved penis, but otherwise, he's wonderful."

Luke

Luke is a 39 year-old Manager and Silicon Valley native. Luke's currently separated from his wife, and in a committed relationship. He enjoys cybersex and describes it as "a great diversion. Its value is directly related to one's use of language, reading skills and imagination."

When asked if he's ever dated anyone he's met online, Luke replied: "Isn't that the goal?"

His best sexual encounter occurred in a motel room, with someone he met online. "One hour after we met online, we met at this motel. We were both so ready to have sex! We ended up doing it for four hours straight. It started with performing oral sex on each other, then I started pumping into her missionary style. Before too long, we ended up doing it doggy-style on the floor. What a great sexual release! We both came several times that day. I was just so ready to have sex and so was she. The timing was perfect!"

Michael

Michael is a 34 year-old web designer who was born and raised in Silicon Valley. He is currently single, and finds dating in Silicon Valley more difficult compared to other areas. He's tried cybersex, and describes it as "not the same, but okay in a pinch."

Twice, he's dated someone he met online. He describes his cybersex meetings: "Once it was great. Once it was BAAAAAD!"

He is still a firm advocate of meeting people online. "I've met some of my best friends, and some good casual lovers online."

Michael's last sexual encounter was a one-night stand, and he rates it an eight out of 10. The details are intriguing: "It was a threesome with two women I met on craigslist," Michael explains. "It was a fun, one-time adventure. It was safe play, just meant to be a fun night. They were both older women who knew what they were doing."

The most unusual place Michael's had sex was at the Shoreline Golf Course in Mountain View. "We were coming back from Tahoe, and we got really horny in the car. We decided we couldn't make it home without having a quickie. We pulled over at the golf course, found a spot to park, and went at it right there in the car. We couldn't have cared less if a bunch of senior citizens in a golf cart drove right by. Biological need definitely overrode any inhibitions about sex in a public place. To this day, I can't drive by that golf course without smiling!"

Patty

Patty is a divorced writer, age 53. Her family moved to the Bay Area 40 years ago from New York. While she dates frequently, her last sexual encounter was somewhat unfulfilling. "It was all good up to the point where this guy did not have a condom. So when he did get my help and had his orgasm, it was indescribable. I'm sure the entire neighborhood heard it."

Her online dating experiences have also left her unfulfilled. Here, she describes a particularly painful experience: "We'd been doing online sex thru emails hot and heavy for two weeks, and phone calls too. I had his picture, he didn't have mine. Seemed to make no difference. We met in San Francisco and when he saw me, he was disgusted. We had a hotel room, he tried to make out with me. I was crazy about him at that point. He got up and said, 'No chemistry here, let's go.' That was it. I dropped him off never to see or hear from him again. And I was just about in love with him."

"Online dating is tough," says Patty. "It hurts to be rejected based on what you look like. I always say to people, 'Remember online is fantasy.' It's never real. When you see the whites of his eyes and he sees yours, that's the reality of it. Nothing more, nothing less."

Although she is currently unattached, she is optimistic about the future. "I am hoping to someday have a really great story and a really great encounter with meaning."

Barbara

Barbara is 35 and works in the legal field. She moved to the Bay Area from New York in 1983. Currently single, she has dabbled in cybersex in the past but found it unfulfilling. "I had cyber sex very often when I first started chatting online. It was enjoyable, but ultimately an empty experience. I want more, so I no longer do it."

Her last sexual partner "had trouble maintaining an erection. He also fumbled a bit, and kept confusing my anus with my vagina. Whether this was on purpose or not, I don't know. Needless to say, there was no repeat performance. I've been with men since him, but have not had intercourse with them (yet)."

Having dated for more than two decades, Barbara definitely has had her share of interesting dates. "I've dated men I met through friends, met in bookstores, hardware stores, at hockey games and, recently, online. I've also tried newspaper personal ads, telephone chat lines, online chat rooms and online personal ads."

Her most unusual encounter took place on a pool table. "I was drunk, and we were both horny. At first I thought it would be uncomfortable, but it wasn't that bad. Pool tables are much stronger than you would think."

Her most bizarre encounter actually never took place: "I chatted with this guy in the SF City Chat room on MSN. After a few minutes, he asked me if we could meet for a drink. He was single, unattached and had just moved to the area from the UK. So I thought to myself, what the heck? We agreed on a location, date and time, and I was just about to say goodbye, when he said, 'Oh there's one thing I forgot to tell you…I have a black dick.'" Since he had previously told her he was Caucasian, Barbara was caught off guard.

"I said, 'What the hell do you mean?' He said, 'Well, women in the UK prefer to have sex with black men, so I had an operation. Now my dick is black. I thought you should know, so you won't be surprised.'" Yeah, that would have been a major surprise.

"All I could think of was that somewhere in England some poor black dude was walking around without a cock!" Barbara says. After overcoming her shock, "I told him I didn't think his comment was funny, and that I would pass. Made me wonder though."

Though that experience was odd, to say the least, it was not Barbara's biggest dating disaster. That particular honor was claimed by a motor mouth with a perverse popcorn fetish. "I had chatted with someone online for several weeks, and we finally agreed to meet face to face. He seemed nice, and our conversations were always pretty tame. Dating online is pretty much a hit or miss gig. I've been stood up a lot, so I don't expect much at first. But, then again, I've also met some really great guys. So, you never know."

They agreed to meet at a sports bar in Palo Alto for a drink where Barbara soon learned she was in for a long evening. "Now, we all have had dates where the other person monopolizes the conversation, but this guy took the cake. I barely got to say two words the entire night. And what did he talk about the whole night? His sexual prowess and vast experience in bed. He told me he had been with more than 40 women, always made them come and couldn't understand why they treated him so badly. (He was divorced twice, something he didn't tell me when we chatted.) He then proceeded to tell me that he'd done threesomes and foursomes and how he once made love for two days straight in a motel room in Vegas. Some women might have been impressed but not me. I kept thinking that his partner probably couldn't even get a word in edgewise the whole week-end, even when she was screaming her climax!"

But his never-ending stream of incredibly boring conversation wasn't the worst part of the evening. "About an hour after listening to this mono-logue, I noticed that the guy had dropped some popcorn onto his fly. (He had been talking with his mouth full the whole night.) I pointed to his pants and said, 'You've got some popcorn there.' We both laughed…until he unzipped his fly and started rubbing himself with it. I just about fell off the barstool!"

Fortunately, they were in the back of the bar where it was dark, so no one saw him. "I couldn't believe it," says Barbara. Especially when he said, "Now it will taste yummy when you give me a blow job tonight." She grabbed her purse and got the hell out of there, leaving him alone with his fly unzipped and popcorn on his cock!

While there have been quite a few bad dates, there have also been good times with great lovers. "One time I had four (count 'em four!) orgasms in one night. The man I was with at the time was REALLY good at foreplay, so two of those orgasms were before penetration. Back rubs, long slow kisses, lots of caresses, neck kissing, heavy petting and oral sex were all part of his seduction. It worked! By the time he was ready to penetrate me, I was practically jumping on him. Very memorable."

Although she has yet to find Mr. Right, Barbara remains optimistic. "What I've learned in more than two decades of dating is that, while the forum may change, basic male-female interaction is the same. There are always nice guys out there, just as there will always be jerks. If you get hit on in real life, you will get hit on online, even more so, though. I think online dating makes people more brazen. So, you just have to be a little more resilient and know what you are looking for. I've not found the right person to spend my life with yet, but I am always hopeful. Call me an optimist. I still believe love is out there for me. I won't settle for anything less."

Don

Don is a 28 year-old man who describes his occupation as laid off, an increasingly common profession in Silicon Valley these days. Don is new to cybersex but definitely intrigued: "My first experience was quite arousing…basically I was telling this girl what I would do to her if I was there! It was quite interesting since I've never tried it before. The anticipation of what the person was going to type next kept the suspense level at its peak. I enjoyed it!"

Don has also enjoyed good luck with finding dates online. He describes a recent online meeting: "We chatted online for a while, and then chatted on the phone for a while. She was from San Diego and told me she was coming to the Bay Area to visit friends and family. We decided to hook up and a relationship began from there. We started dating, and that led to some very good sex!"

Larry

Larry, a self-described "software geek," is 40 and lives in the South Bay. He is divorced and involved in a casual relationship. He says he has met "a lot of partners on online dating boards," however, he has not tried cybersex. "I don't go in for one-handed typing. But I have exchanged a few stories."

"Meeting people online, I go on a lot more first dates than second," says Larry. "One woman described herself as cute and slightly overweight, when she was actually ugly and obese. I met her for dinner, she brought along her eight year-old son (which I expected) who turned out to be an absolute monster. Needless to say, there was no second date.

But, I have learned a lot, too, from meeting people online. Someone I met on one of the dating boards was having trouble, being harassed by one guy in particular. I joked that I could create a woman's account and seriously flame him. She took me seriously and begged me to do it. So, I did.

Being online as a woman was very educational. I realized how bad the majority of emails that guys send girls actually is! It was a serious wakeup call."

Larry offers the following tips and tricks to make online dating more successful: "First off, after you meet someone online, proceed to phone conversations and a first meeting as quickly as possible. It's important to establish if there really is any chemistry. Over emails, folks often come across as perfect, but when you meet them in person, you quickly find out you don't have much in common.

Also, spelling counts, as does writing ability. If someone makes a lot of spelling mistakes, they come off as a total idiot. Short notes that just say 'write to me,' 'check out my profile' or 'wanna have sex?' also don't cut it."

Chapter Three

The Best Sex Ever

Our survey respondents were asked to describe their "best sex ever." Many of their encounters are included with their stories in other areas of the book. But a couple of survey respondents provided so much amazing (and delectable) detail on their encounters that we've featured them here as their own chapter: *The Best Sex Ever*.

*   *   *

Katie

Katie, is 25 and originally from the Southwest. Her most amazing sexual encounter occurred on a rock, with the help of a dripping orange. Here are the 'juicy' details:

"I lived near a lake and visited there often to cool off on hot, hot sunny days. One beautiful day, I was sunning on a rock, and thoroughly enjoying eating a fresh, juicy orange.

On the rock next to me, there was a cute guy, also sunning himself. Feeling flirtatious, I offered him some of my orange. He accepted it with a gorgeous smile, and we started to talk. In no time at all, we were sharing the same rock, laughing, and touching."

One thing led to another between Katie and her sunbathing partner. "We had the most amazing sex, right there in the sunshine. I remember it so clearly. I was looking up at the shady trees overhead, while his body slid in and out of me. We had sticky orange residue all over us. It was the best sex I've ever had. Hot, explosive, exciting. I didn't ask his name. I didn't want to know, and I never saw him again."

When asked what her ideal sexual encounter would be, Katie replied with a smile: "I wouldn't mind finding that guy again, and offering him another piece of my orange."

Faith

Faith submitted this story in its entirety. She calls this story *Are You Ready?*

Faith: "It had been 14 months since a man had touched me. An ugly ending to a long relationship left me fearful of any encounters. My ex wasn't into sex: he never could get fully hard, would deflate as soon as the condom appeared, and was really boring in bed. So not only had it been a long time since an encounter of any kind, but a good encounter—it had been YEARS! Any encounter at this point of my life would have qualified as the best encounter...

At a web design conference in New York, during an evening event, I sat down next to an empty chair and a pile of books. When the owner returned, I was pleasantly surprised. He was sexy. I'm pretty charismatic, so it wasn't hard to get his card. His card said he was a web designer (just like me) in San Francisco. I worked in Cupertino. Perfect!

I spent the next day at the conference with him and then we went out drinking. Standing in the middle of Times Square at 3:00 in the morning, he asked about my love life. I explained my lack of a man situation and the ugly breakup. He was so sensitive about it all, full of positive words and a huge hug, that I was starting to think that I might let this man break my dry spell.

He didn't want a girlfriend and I didn't want a boyfriend. I was having a hard time trying to let myself go and just make out with the guy. I'm not a hook-up girl at all. I'd rather masturbate than be hurt, so it's easier to say no and not even get let my body get too close to someone because I don't have much restraint once in a heavy-breathing situation.

He was way too smooth skinned and sexy for me not to at least make out with. He had my back pressed against a darkened wall next to my hotel, and before he kissed me, he whispered 'Are you ready?' I said, 'Yes.' And he said, 'If you can't kiss, it's all over.'

I am pressed up against the wall, and he bends over and kisses me. He's holding one hand next to my side and the other is holding my face. I had electricity shooting out of me. I felt it right in my crotch. I could have been 16 again. I got SO WET—in like seconds! I could barely breathe. I was breathing heavy and practically moaning. I had to catch my breath. His tongue was so fierce. He kissed me like he was having sex with my mouth. I was really turned on when he pressed his crotch up against mine and he had a hard on—my God! I hadn't felt that in over a year!

I kissed him some more. I really was so turned on. I told him I was on fire, that I felt it 'right there' and put my hand on my crotch. He smiled and says, 'Right there, huh?' So he grabbed me and mashed me really close and said something about getting my chest really close to him. I said, 'It's just a bra. I don't have any boobs—I have really cute nipples, though.' And he puts his hand on the wall above my head, exhales and says, 'Do you feel that?' Referring to his crotch. I said, 'Yes.' He said, 'My **** is about to poke through the wall.'

After some more kissing and almost being mugged (no kidding!), he walked me down to the hotel and left. I was sharing the room with a friend, or I would have ripped my clothes off and masturbated as soon as I walked in. I was pulling off my underwear, and it was soaking wet. My crotch was POUNDING. I wanted to masturbate so badly, but I knew if I did, the walls would shake and I would make a ton of noise.

After I slept for an hour, I woke up and couldn't get back to sleep. I was fantasizing and remembering how he kissed.

Back at home in the Silicon Valley, I spent the next 10 days in masturbation hell. I knew that a man who kissed like that could give me some fantastic oral sex. I kept asking myself if I thought that I could rip his clothes off without liking him too much. I decided to take that risk. I just couldn't physically handle my hormones anymore.

When I called him, I said hello and so did he. The next sentence from me was, 'Remember, when I said that I would love to go get naked with you, but not when I'm drunk? Well, when do you want to go get naked?'

He was all over that invitation.

I couldn't sleep that night, or any other night when I talked to him on the phone. Each phone call had me peeling off my clothes little by little from the hot flashes I would get remembering what he felt like and what I wanted to happen. I would be in my underwear by the time the phone call ended and I wouldn't sleep all night.

We finally set a date, and I couldn't wait. And he proved to be as hot as I expected. I remember getting up off the bed and him and taking my pants off to show off my sassy purple panties with clip off sides—so sexy! He was laying on the bed and as I'm getting back on top of him he looks at the ceiling and says 'Thank You, God.' Now THAT, has got to be the most awesome thing I have ever heard when getting naked with someone.

He worshipped my body with compliments and touches. We had hours of grinding and touching—I had more orgasms than I can remember. He licked, kissed, and bit spots that would pop up anywhere near his mouth. He attacked everything the same way he kissed. I knew he would be this way, and this was exactly what I wanted.

Okay, so he goes down on me, and I thought for sure, I was going to faint. But first he asked me, "Are you ready?"—as if he had to ask! I'd been wet for hours…and hours… and I can still see him asking me, and the look on his face, like I should prepare. And really, I should have. Because there it was—there's that kiss—the same kiss I get on my mouth—but on a much sweeter spot.

I couldn't stop thinking how good of a choice I had made for the guy who got to be my first sexual encounter since my ex. I wasn't planning on having intercourse with him, just lots of everything else. But I couldn't resist, I knew I would regret it if I didn't.

So, after an hour of awesome sex, he asks me again before he's ready to come, 'Are you ready?' I tell him I am. I am, but, I can honestly say, I could have kept on having sex.

We hadn't left the bedroom yet and it's 2:00 in the afternoon. We're both hungry, but sex is taking over the real hunger for me. I could care less. I haven't had coffee or anything. I didn't put any makeup on, and this guy thinks I'm beautiful and is screwing my brains out all the while worshipping my body—why would I want to 'be ready?'

The experience left me bleeding for four days. I laughed every time I wiped after using the restroom. I emailed my girlfriends and told them I was bleeding from not having sex in so long—you can imagine how much fun they had with that one.

I've seen him since one other time to have sex. I've also seen him twice not to have sex. The two non-sex visits left me sweating and nervous. I can't seem to stop thinking about his sexual techniques, and he has this habit of licking the sides of his mouth with his tongue, which makes my crotch throb, so I can't look at him when he does that. I can't really look at him much in general, because I get so excited in his presence. It's animal attraction. Pure and raw stuff. A couple months ago I saw someone walking away from me through a parking lot and I was mesmerized. I walked faster trying to see who the man was, he walked liked he owned the City. In a matter of seconds, I realized, it was Him.

I like men again, but I don't find many people 'my type' – whatever that is. If a man comes on to me really sexually, I turn into an ice queen and shut him down. And the sort of person I am attracts this sort of person.

Here it is, almost another year since a man has touched me AGAIN. There's another factor to add into the equation here, I am now in my mid thirties, and my desire for sex has been increasing. Whether this is from the lack of touch or just my age, I don't know yet.

So far, that was the best sex I ever had. I sometimes think I should send him a thank you card.

Sam

Sam, 32, a Human Resources Manager, enjoyed his best sexual encounter ever on a broiling summer day. "I was an undergraduate attending college in Denton, Texas. It was a hot day, easily over 100 degrees, and a good friend of mine, a lady friend, had come over to my room.

We were talking, and laughing, and enjoying each other's company. One thing led to another, and before you know it, our clothes were off and we were touching each other everywhere. It was obvious she wanted sex, and I was more than willing to oblige. A few days before, I'd changed some of the light bulbs in the room to red bulbs, and now I had the perfect opportunity to try them out.

I put on Pink Floyd's 'Dark Side of the Moon' and I pumped into her with the red light streaming all over us. The sweat just lubricated us more, and we slapped against each other's bodies, making a lot of noise about it, until we both finally came.

It was one of those hot, sweaty situations that you read about in the back pages of magazines—except it was better because it was real!

Even though it's been 10 years since that encounter, my friend still e-mails me whenever she hears Pink Floyd on the radio!"

Another memorable encounter occurred at the Royal Melbourne Institute of Technology.

"I was going to school in Melbourne, Australia, and during the first week of school, there was a street party. I met a nice girl. After a few drinks, we both started getting amorous.

So, we sneaked into the men's room in the Student Union. There were some showers there, so we headed into the showers, and had wonderful sex pressed up against the tile walls.

Getting this girl into the bathroom had been easy, but getting her back out again proved very difficult. The bathroom was within sight of the

Institute's Administrative Offices. The secretary had a keen eye on me. She didn't know what I was doing, but she did know I was up to no good. Fortunately, she finally turned her back long enough that I was able to sneak my lovemaking partner out of the men's room and back out to the street party."

Sandy & James

Sandy moved to Silicon Valley five years ago, leaving behind her family, her job, and everything she'd known. "I just needed a change from New York," says Sandy. "I was only planning on staying out here two years. I was going to get some good job experience, and then move back to New York."

"I almost felt pressure to find somebody out here. Pressure from my Mom," Sandy says, "When I'd left for California, my Mom had said: 'Sandy, if you don't find a husband out there in Silicon Valley, there's no hope for you.'"

"Mom's words just stuck in my head," said Sandy, "with all the single men out here, shouldn't men be beating down my door looking to go out with me? But sadly, that wasn't the case."

For the first year Sandy lived in the Bay Area, her dating life was stale and uneventful.

"I guess maybe I was setting my standards too high. I don't know. But I just didn't seem to be meeting anyone I'd want to seriously date. The guys who asked me out weren't people I wanted to date, and the ones I was interested in were all attached, or not looking to date. Things didn't look good," says Sandy.

And then, they got worse. The startup company Sandy worked for went bankrupt, owing all employees months of backpay and unpaid expenses.

"I was so desperately broke," said Sandy. "While I was job hunting, I relieved stress by going to the beach in Santa Cruz. I started body boarding, because it was cheap, and easy to learn. But then, one day, I borrowed someone's surfboard and tried surfing. I was instantly hooked. Catching my first wave was the greatest feeling in the world. I started surfing every day. Plus, it relaxed and focused me to the point that my job interviews started going much better. I felt I was close to a couple of different job offers."

And then, life got even more interesting for Sandy.

"It was a beautiful Sunday morning and I'd been surfing since dawn," says Sandy. "I was about to call it a day when this gorgeous guy paddled right by me. His muscles were rippling in his wetsuit, and he had the most incredible eyes, I was instantly intrigued by him, and decided I had to stay to at least see him catch one wave."

Sandy later learned the surfer was named James. James picks up the story from there.

"As I paddled out, I noticed a cute blonde lounging on her surfboard. She smiled at me as I paddled by. I really wanted to catch her attention," says James.

James caught the first wave that came along, not even waiting his turn in the line-up.

"Show off," thought Sandy, watching him paddle for the wave. James caught the wave easily, with a few swift strokes. His lithe body moved as one with the surf. Sandy's jaw dropped as he surfed right by her.

"He was like a Hawaiian Surf God come to life!" says Sandy, "I was so turned on!"

After dropping off the wave, James paddled over to Sandy and struck up a conversation.

"We discussed surfboards, the weather, the wave conditions, anything," said James, "I just wanted to keep her talking. I was trying to work up the nerve to ask her out to lunch. She had the greatest smile. I just got such a good vibe from her."

The two quickly discovered they had much in common. They both lived and worked in Silicon Valley for high-tech companies, both loved the outdoors, both enjoyed playing guitar, and both had a passionate love for the ocean and surfing.

"We surfed side by side until the waves were completely dead," says Sandy, "And then casual as can be James said: 'I was just going to get some lunch. Perhaps you'd like to join me?' Normally, I wouldn't accept an invite like that from a stranger, but some deep instinct within me told me to say 'Yes!'"

They put their surfboards away, and headed to lunch in James' sleek little convertible.

"All through lunch, I kept thinking: 'I really want to kiss this guy,'" admits Sandy. "Although, I must admit I was distracted by this hole in my pants. We were having lunch outdoors at this cute little beachside place. Because I was unemployed, I hadn't bought new clothes in a while. The pair of jogging pants I was wearing was pretty ragged. There was a pretty noticeable hole in the crotch, which wouldn't have mattered if I had just gone straight home after surfing. But here I am, on a first date with a great guy, with a pair of pants with a big hole in the crotch, and nothing on underneath. (Surfer's traditionally don't bother with underwear.) Showing a nice stretch of *poonani* wasn't the impression I wanted to make on a first date!"

James didn't notice. His mind was distracted wondering how he could get Sandy to go out on a second date with him. If Sandy was distracted by the breeze between her legs, James was distracted trying to think of how to get this appealing blonde to go on a second date with him.

At James' suggestion, they took a long walk together on the beach after lunch, and then James drove Sandy back to her car.

"We exchanged e-mail addresses, and agreed to have dinner that Thursday," said Sandy, "I was thrilled he wanted a second date with me, but disappointed that he didn't invite me back to his place right away. I know this will sound totally slutty, but I was sooooo turned on by him, that I was willing to throw all caution to the wind. Every nerve in my body was totally alive. I wanted so much to kiss him, to touch him, to be naked next to him. I was literally on fire, just being near him."

The two exchanged a brief hug and then headed their separate ways.

Sandy headed home, her mind totally focused on James.

"I was so turned on that I had to masturbate before I could even go to bed that night," said Sandy, "I've never been that attracted to a guy before. I felt as if something very, very special had happened to me that day."

James was feeling the same way.

"I couldn't stop thinking about Sandy," says James. "On Monday, I couldn't concentrate at work. All I could think is 'I have to see this girl again, and Thursday is too long to wait!' I e-mailed her and asked if we could move our dinner date to that night. She was tied up with a late afternoon job interview, but we agreed to have dinner Tuesday night. I was thrilled."

James arrived at Sandy's apartment on Tuesday evening to take her out to a restaurant for dinner.

"When I arrived, she'd surprised me by having prepared this nice dinner, everything homemade, and complete with flowers on the table. It was very romantic. After dinner, we headed out to a movie. It was 'How Stella Got Her Groove Back.' There was a lot of sex in the movie and I was very turned on by the time we got out of the theater. When I dropped her off back at her apartment, I was faced with a dilemma. Do I invite myself in, or would that seem too forward? I didn't want to ruin anything, as I really liked this girl. But Sandy ended my dilemma very quickly by inviting me in."

Sandy picks up the story from there: "I told James that I always watch Star Trek at 10:00 p.m. and asked if he'd like to watch it with me. He said: 'Yes! Love the show!' Turns out, he hates Star Trek, and if it wasn't for 7 of 9's huge breasts, he still wouldn't watch the show at all. But, all that's history now. The important thing is he came into the apartment."

In just a few minutes, the TV show was forgotten and Sandy was on the floor with her panties around her knees.

"We were very heavily kissing and petting each other," says Sandy, "we were both so turned on. The sexual tension had been building for two days and we both felt it. I was so ready to go all the way, but James wanted to hold back. He was actually very sweet.

He could see I was about bursting out of my skin, and he went down on me, giving me about the best oral sex I've ever had. I came so hard I bucked up off the carpet. It was amazing. I was completely wiped out afterwards. James gently lead me to my bed, tucked me in, and said: 'I'll see you Thursday night for our original dinner date.'

"I was amazed at his restraint, as he definitely could have had me. I was so into him. But he wanted to wait, so it would be even more special. I slept so soundly that night. I felt so totally at peace, as if one of the most important pieces of my life had just clicked into place. And, as it turned out, it did."

On Thursday night, James made Sandy a candlelight dinner at his house. They talked, laughed, and after a thoroughly satisfying meal, ended up in the bedroom.

"The moment our bodies finally connected, and we were making love, I knew something very, very special was happening," says Sandy.

"I've never meant anyone like Sandy," says James, "from the very beginning, it was pure magic between us."

Six months later, Sandy and James were engaged. Other things fell into place for Sandy, too. She landed a great job with another startup, and this one ended up going all the way to a very successful IPO.

"True love is out there," says James, "but it's important not to settle. When you meet the right woman, you will know. Everything just clicks into place."

Chapter Four

Chick Who Prefer Chicks and Other Tales

The Bay Area has long been known as a haven for same-sex couples seeking sexual freedom and acceptance. Not surprisingly, our survey respondents included a generous mix of same-sex and bisexual couples, sharing their stories and adventures.

*   *   *

Chyna

Chyna is a 25 year-old female, originally from Oakland, who works in Audio/Video production. She made the move across the Bay "for money." She is single, describes her single status as "swinging," and is very confident about both her physical appearance, and her sexual prowess.

An exotic mixture of Ethiopian and Puerto Rican, Chyna has almost pinup-perfect stats of 36-24-36. She is openly bisexual, although hasn't been with a woman for the past three months. "That's a long stretch for me," says Chyna.

Her last sexual encounter was with a female friend, who Chyna did not know was curious about trying a same-sex encounter. The two went drinking, and ended up at a strip club.

Chyna picks up the story: "We were at a strip club in San Francisco. I paid for her to have a lap dance and she loved it. After the lap dance, she was a little more open and excited. We quickly headed back to my place. We ended up having oral sex, totally licking each other until we each climaxed. I shiver now just thinking about it! She is now openly bisexual and has a girlfriend. But, she still makes frequent visits to my place, usually around 2:00 a.m., so I guess I'm pretty good at what I do!"

One of Chyna's most memorable sexual experiences involved oral sex in an apartment hallway. "Last summer, on July 7th, I went to pick up a friend of mine from the airport. I thought she was straight, but when we met at the airport, she gave me a good solid kiss. A more than friends sort of kiss. She says she wants to head back to her place, take a shower and 'chill out.' As we're driving there, she asks if I thought she was sexy. I answered: 'Hell, yeah! You look Golden!' When we got to her place, she licked my ear in the elevator on the way up. We got out of the elevator, and walked to her door. She pushed me up against the wall, and kissed me like crazy. Then, she grabbed under my skirt and ripped my undies off. I screamed with surprise. She laughed, and dropped to her knees, right there in the hallway!

She performed incredible oral sex on me, sticking her tongue between my spread legs and sucking at my clit. I then returned the favor, still there in the hallway!

Just as we were finishing, we heard the elevator bell ding. It was her mom coming by to see if she made it home safe!

We quickly played off what we were doing, and I guess her mom bought it, as she left after a short visit.

Once the mom was gone, we stayed in her apartment for three days pleasuring each other!"

But Chyna doesn't limit her sexual talents to just women. "I was out with a guy I had been seeing for about four months," says Chyna, "We liked to go 'lady hunting' together at clubs. It made our sex life more interesting. Well, one night at a club, we met with three girls that were all 'together.' They were 24, 28 and 30 and wanted a piece of my boy. I let them know that I came with the package, too. It ended up being the most beautiful experience I've ever had! Imagine legs, arms, lips, hands, and fingers times five... What could be better!"

When asked about her ideal sexual scenario, Chyna says: "Me, twelve women, and one man, all out to please me!"

Stephanie

Stephanie is 24, single, and loves women. She moved to the Bay Area from Southern California three years ago. She enjoys having sex with her female co-workers, and her most unusual encounter was in the copy room at work.

"Last summer my boss's daughter was working as an intern," Stephanie says, "She was always walking around in tight skirts and low cut blouses. We were working late and she came up to me and asked for help with the copying machine. When I arrived in the copy room, she closed and locked the door. She turned to me, and told me how much she wanted me. We ended up going down on each other, leaning right up against the copy equipment! It was wild!

We ended up having sex through the rest of the summer. She was a fun girl. I hope she decides to do another internship next summer..."

Stephanie says she enjoys being attracted to a woman who at first might seem out of reach, and then "having the woman come on to me."

Stephanie concludes: "Most of the girls in San Francisco and Silicon Valley who you think are straight, are actually totally into girls if given the chance!"

Steve

Steve is a 27 year-old straight male, originally from Portland, Oregon. We've included Steve in the same sex and bisexual chapter due to his recent experimentation with same-sex partners.

"Although I am straight, I have experimented with same sex activities," says Steve. "The only real action I've had with other guys is oral sex, mutual masturbation and a couple of forays into anal sex. I didn't care much for the anal sex. Truth be told, I haven't had sex with a woman since I moved here. In my experience, guys give better head than girls."

When asked if he's tried cybersex, Steve replied: "Lately, cybersex is about the only sex I have. But, it's not so bad. I have great orgasms with cybersex. I can chat for hours, while hard. When I finally orgasm, it's long and intense."

Joe

Joe is a 41 year-old gay male, originally from Orange County. He moved to the Bay Area for a better job, and is currently living with a partner.

He describes the challenges of dating here: "This is a very hard place to make friends. There is not any organization or central meeting place. No outlets but work. The area is actually very traditional and uptight for all its celebrated relaxed attitudes."

His last sexual encounter was "very enjoyable for both of us. The only bad thing was that our dogs were restless outside, and that interrupted our play."

The most unusual place Joe has enjoyed a sexual encounter is in a Los Angeles party bar. "Mmmm... the details? It was a gathering at a party bar. Lots of dark areas. Me and two other guys were interested in each other so we found a dark corner and took care of each other. It was fun and we had spectators!"

Now, at age 41, Joe is happily settled into a committed relationship with his partner, and Joe describes their sex as "the best sex ever."

Ed

Ed is a 41 year-old gay male who works in the non-profit Social Services sector. Ed is originally from New Hampshire and came to Silicon Valley for the "sexual freedom, job market, and climate."

Ed is currently single, but stresses he is "NOT alone. Strong, multiple friendships." Ed's enjoyed over 10 dates in the past month, and 10 sexual encounters.

"I've never found dating difficult," says Ed. "I'm secure with myself, not into restrictions, and am pretty vocal about going after what interests me."

Ed's tried cybersex but says: "I'll only do it with the right person. They must be talented enough to want to make me type with one hand!" Ed's met up in person with some of his cybersex partners but says: "only one has ever lived up his 'cyber profile.'" He has, however, met sex partners online "many, many times. Most of my hook-ups are from the Internet."

Ed's most recent sexual encounter was a one-night stand that rated a perfect 10. "The man I was with was a gentleman... what a surprise!" says Ed. "He was very attentive to my body language, and I to his. We were both intent on satisfying each other, not just ourselves. What was to be a quick trick turned into an all-nighter. It's nice now and then to be surprised to want to fall asleep in a stranger's arms... who no longer feels like a stranger."

When asked about the most unusual place he's had sex, Ed commented: "Geez! What memories! My friend Matthew and I used to play a game called 'Dare.' We would dare each other to have sex together in public places where we were taking a risk of getting caught. Once, we had sex on a rooftop at our conservative college campus. We were actually watched by a security guard who fondled himself to completion. We also had sex once where I was bent over a gravestone in a cemetery. Other places included public buses, phone booths, locker rooms, at public beaches, etc."

As for the best sex ever, Ed says: "It's still going on! Do we ever have the best? What would be left to strive for?"

Elvis

Elvis is a 21 year-old male, originally from Fresno, California, who describes his occupation as "not available." (We're assuming this means Elvis is currently between jobs.)

Elvis finds dating here "extremely easy, but I'm not one for jumping in the sack too soon."

Elvis' last sexual encounter was in the past week, with a dating partner. Elvis rates it a six out of 10. "Both of us were too nervous and inexperienced," says Elvis, "But, once that wore off, it was HOT!"

Elvis' most unusual encounter happened under the Bay Bridge. "On Yerba Buena Island, there is a small road that crosses under the Bay Bridge... I thought, what a way to celebrate PRIDE... holding on to a chain linked metal fence having sex under the gay Mecca of the world... Totally out in the open, naked ass in the cool night air... It doesn't get any better than that."

Like many of our survey respondents, Elvis' best sexual encounter involved a situation where he could have been caught at anytime, thus heightening the thrill and intensity of the encounter. "My best sex was receiving a blowjob from my boyfriend, while his stepmother was in the next room with the door open... Totally hot in the sense that his mom could have walked in on us at any moment!"

Chapter Five

Auto-Erotica (no, it's not about cars)

While masturbation is probably universally popular the world over, it's a great stress reliever for the overworked singles of the Valley. When there's no time for dating, or the dates just aren't coming (no pun intended), a little bit of self-sufficiency can go a long way.

While masturbation seems to come naturally to men, it often takes longer for women to figure out how to masturbate successfully to completion. But with enough time and imagination, women, too, can gain the upper hand (pun intended).

*   *   *

Roxanne

Roxanne, 29, moved to San Jose from Boston three years ago. While she enjoys her job as a Public Relations Manager for a chip manufacturer, she hasn't had much luck at the dating scene.

"I've dated two different guys out here," says Roxanne, "only one of which I even ended up going so far as to have sex with. And, sadly, the sex wasn't very good. He didn't really know what he was doing, and while he always seemed to enjoy it, I didn't get much satisfaction from it."

Then, Roxanne discovered satisfaction from a most unlikely source.

"It was the day I moved into my new apartment," says Roxanne, " I was hot and sweating after unpacking boxes all day. I decided to shower, and discovered the shower had a pull-down, massaging showerhead. I soaped up all over, pulled the showerhead off its little holder, and began trying the massaging action out all over. It felt great on the tired muscles of my back, my neck, my arms, my legs. Well, I'd soaped up all over, including between my legs, so I aimed the massaging showerhead down there to get a good rinsing."

It was then that Roxanne discovered the hidden benefits of the shower in her new apartment.

"The moment that massaging showerhead was aimed between my legs, I began to feel it," says Roxanne. "The spray of water from the massaging showerhead was hitting my clitoris. The little bud of my clitoris came out of its hiding place and I was fully aroused. I wondered if I could orgasm just from a showerhead? I decided to find out. I spread my legs a little wider and positioned the water just right. Then, I just totally relaxed and let it happen. I felt this delicious, incredible sense of tension building, first between my legs, and then in the pit of my stomach. The orgasm came upon me so quickly! I can only describe the sensation as one thousand watery tongues licking my clitoris all at once! It was a frenzy of watery excitement. I just loved it! I just exploded. The orgasm was so intense that my knees buckled, I dropped the showerhead, and I had to hold on to the walls of the shower to keep from falling."

When Roxanne emerged from the shower she felt not only super clean, but sexually refreshed and satisfied. "It was such a quick, clean enjoyable orgasm," said Roxanne, "I've never felt anything like it. No man has ever made me feel like that. And sadly, I'm not sure if they could. How can you compete with the combined licking force of a thousand watery tongues?"

Roxanne still hopes to meet the right man, settle down and start a family. "But no matter where I live, I'll make sure we install a massaging shower head into the bathroom," says Roxanne. "That way, I know I'll always be sexually satisfied no matter what. My husband could turn out to be a wonderful guy who's only an average lover, and I'll still be satisfied. Mr. Showerhead will see to that."

Debbie

Debbie is a 32 year-old Communications Manager for a networking company. She first had sex when she was 14, in her boyfriend's car. But, it took another seven years before she even discovered that such a thing as 'orgasm' existed.

"I guess my boyfriends in high school were as clueless as I was when it came to woman's orgasms. I just thought that sex felt sort of good, but never knew there this was this incredible peak of sensation known as orgasm. Over the course of high school, I dated three different guys. After we'd dated for a month or two, we'd always inevitably progress from groping and petting to full-out intercourse. I was driven to have sex because, like all teenagers, I had a lot of hormones raging through my body. Having sex eased the horniness for a while. I surprised to hear some women were nymphomaniacs, and were addicted to the great feelings that sex produced. Other than easing the overload of teenage hormones rampaging through my body, I couldn't see what was so great about sex that you'd get hooked on it.

After graduating high school, I went on to attend a college that was very good academically, but a disaster with regards to the dating scene. There were six women for every guy there! Needless to say, I didn't date nearly as much in college as high school. So, sexually it was a pretty dry spell. I dated one guy my sophomore year but it didn't last long and we never had sex. After a while, I just learned to deal with celibacy. I didn't masturbate, as I didn't really know how. I just did without, although I was prone to eating ice chips, as I still did get horny sometimes.

Then, when I was 21, I had a most interesting conversation with a female college friend. She asked: 'How old were you when you had your first orgasm?'

I asked her what she meant. I'd heard of the word, but it didn't hold much meaning for me.

She looked at me skeptically: 'You mean, you've never had one? Not even by yourself?'

I didn't want to seem like I was totally naive, so I said: 'Well, maybe I have. It's not like I haven't had sex. I had boyfriends in high school. What exactly does an orgasm feel like?'

She described it to me in great detail. I listened with widened eyes, and she could tell I'd never had one just by my reaction.

'You can have one by yourself,' she reassured me, 'It's the best way to get to know your body. You don't need a guy for that.'

'Tell me more,' I pleaded.

'Just keeping touching yourself, until it feels really good, and then don't stop. Reading romance novels helps. They often describe orgasms in great detail, plus they are great for getting women horny. Once you've had an orgasm, you will know it, trust me. Just keep experimenting.'

After that conversation, I made it my mission to have a first orgasm. I bought some romance novels, and found that they did indeed describe the sensation in great detail. I'd moved off-campus at that point, and had my own room, so I had plenty of privacy for self-experimentation.

The romance novels were great for turning me on, and making me eager to experiment with touching myself. I became a voracious reader, going through at least a novel a week.

It was just a few short months later that I finally figured it out, and masturbated myself to my first orgasm. The feeling was incredible! I remember shaking afterwards, and being filled with a sense of wonder that I never knew such a thing existed.

It took no time at all before I became very, very good at touching myself in all the right places, and bring myself to orgasm. I started having them several times a week.

I became hooked on both masturbation, and reading romance novels for years after that. I got very, very good at giving myself an orgasm.

I didn't give them up until years later when I ended up marrying a lover so good that it was like living the romance novel. (No kidding! This guy rocks my world!)

But, I don't think my love life now would be nearly so good if I hadn't learned how to masturbate and bring myself to orgasm while in college. Once you know how to please yourself, it's much easier to coach your lover in how to please you. Enjoyable sex with a partner is a process of experimentation, trust and open-communication. The first step is definitely: 'Know Thyself.'"

Joseph

Joseph is a 32 year-old Construction worker, originally from Atlanta, Georgia. He is currently "in and out of relationship with a girl I want to marry, but since she can't 'figure it out', I guess I'm sometimes single. I hope she figures it out, so I can marry her!"

Joseph's best sexual encounter involved his girlfriend and a vibrator. "My current girlfriend and I have this amazing sexual connection—the best either one of us have ever had. We go for hours just enjoying each other's company, exploring our bodies, until we just have to have an orgasm or we'll explode. One day, my girlfriend pulls a small vibrator from her purse and asks me if I'd mind using it on her. I gladly accept the invitation, as I'd never used one before. She had a very intense orgasm, her body shaking and quivering. She was so intense from her orgasm, it took her a good two to three minutes just to come down from it.

As soon as she was able, she started giving me head, and introduced the little vibrator to the region between my scrotum and my anus. As she grew more intense with giving me great head, she would turn the intensity of the vibrator up. Just as I was about to have an earth shattering orgasm, she stops, much to my surprise!

She lays me down, straddles me, and starts rubbing my penis against her pussy. I thought to myself: 'I'm going to explode right now! No, no, not yet, think of something else!' I'm able to hold on for a few more moments, as she slowly inserts me, sliding down on me all the way to the hilt. She stayed there moving her hips in every direction, with this incredible downward pressure.

There she sits, me buried deep inside her, the warmth, the wetness (more like soaked!), and the wonderful smell of sex in the air.

She turns the vibrator on, places it at the base of my penis, and turns my penis into a vibrator for her! I hold the vibrator in place so she can use her arms to thrust her body up and down. She says to me: 'Hang on sweetness!' and wham! she explodes into orgasm, squeezing me and squeezing me. The pressure causes me to explode with her and we have the most shattering orgasms.

I've never had so many body parts of mine go numb at one time!"

Angela

Angela is a 29 year-old Marketing Manager who has definite preferences when it comes to vibrators.

"Forget the battery-operated vibrators. The best kind plug into the wall," says Angela. "I've been using a back massager for the past five years to get me off, and I really did originally buy it for my back. One day I just happened to notice the vibrating action worked really well in other areas, too. My orgasms are so intense, that I'll call my husband at work and tell him: 'You are not going to believe the orgasm I just had! I'm really good at this!' He often finds an excuse to come home early…"

Katherine

Katherine is a 32 year-old Accounting Manager, who just recently discovered the joy of vibrators.

"After my divorce, friends suggested I get a vibrator to ease my sexual frustration," says Katherine. "It took me a while to find one that worked for me, but then I discovered this amazing piece of engineering called 'The Beyond 2000.' I'm embarrassed to say that I've burnt out the 'tickler' on the Beyond 2000 not once, but twice! Their customer service people are wonderful, and keep sending me replacement units, but I think they are beginning to wonder…"

Chapter Six

Dating Disasters

Every survey respondent was asked to include their biggest dating disaster. The respondents appearing here are also featured throughout the book. After reading all these tales of dating woes, it's reassuring to know that everyone's had at least one dating experience they wish they could forget. The important lesson seems to be to pick up the shattered pieces of your dignity, move on, and try again. The lessons learned from today's dating disaster just might lead to tomorrow's dating success. Here are their stories.

*   *   *

"I MADE A DATE WITH A GUY that I had interviewed on the phone for a market survey. I had never met him, but he sounded great on the phone. He came to pick me up for dinner, and insisted we have sex right there on the living room floor, unless I wanted to 'actually go through with having dinner first.' I immediately threw him out, giving the door a good slam the moment he made it through.

It was the shortest date I ever had."

Maggie, 48

"WHEN I FIRST MOVED TO SAN FRANCISCO, I met a girl online. She invited me to her house for a dinner party. Since I just had arrived from Texas, I didn't know a thing about how difficult parking is in San Francisco, particularly near her house in North Beach. I found the address okay and right on time, but it took me over an hour to find a parking place. I circled around and around, looking for a spot. Finally, I found what I thought was a legal parking space, and parked.

I hurried to her apartment. By that point, I had to pee like you wouldn't believe. So, after introducing myself to her, and her house full of friends, I immediately ran to her bathroom. Once I emerged, I asked her if she would lean out the window to see if I was parked legally. (Turns out, I wasn't.) As she leaned out, her favorite potted house plant fell out the window, smashed to the ground and broke.

The evening just continued to get worse from there. They had been holding dinner for me, and an hour late, it wasn't much good anymore. I stayed on for as long as I could, but finally I had to leave in shame. Needless to say, the girl never responded to another email of mine."

Sam, 32

"I WAS ONCE DATING TWO GUYS at the same time. They both thought they were the only ones. I couldn't make up my mind between them and they both were good in bed. So, I figured: 'Why not?' It sure was fun while it lasted, but it ended much too soon...One night I'm out to dinner with one of my boyfriends, and we ran into the other boyfriend. It was typical sitcom stuff. I'm obviously on a date with the one, when the other loudly demands what's going on.

It was a Japanese restaurant, and the two of them suddenly created a very big scene, finally both storming out of there. I was left sitting there alone, with a roomful of Japanese patrons just staring at me. I made a rather quick retreat myself after that, my head hung low, not meeting the eyes of anyone there. I went from having two boyfriends to none, all in one night."

Katie, 25

"MY BIGGEST DATING DISASTER happened with this girl I had just started seeing. I knew she'd been through a big breakup with her ex-boyfriend, but things were going okay between us. We'd reached the point of our relationship where we were ready to have sex.

So, one night, we undress each other, start kissing, and then start going at it. In the middle of sex, she freaks out, telling me we have to stop. I pull out and ask her what's going on. 'We can't do this!' she cries, 'My ex-boyfriend might find out we're having sex!' She asked me to leave, and I did, leaving both her, and her baggage, behind for good."

Joseph, 32

"I WAS AT A COLLEGE in western Massachusetts where there are five schools within five miles of one another. It was wintertime, and I was invited to a party at the 'jock dorm' of another university by a very cute hockey player boy named Joel (not his real name—actually, I don't remember his real name).

I decided to wear my best tan, slightly baggy pants and leather ankle boots—thank you Madonna for the great fashions you created in the late 80s.

Joel and I were walking towards the dorm, which was downhill from the main campus area. It was already very snowy and cold in New England, and the sidewalks were covered in ice. At some point in our stroll, my little boots hit an ice patch. I've never been a skier, but I somehow managed to stay upright as I slid all the way down the hill. I was screaming, and my arms were flailing, the whole way.

Finally, about 50 feet down the hill, I managed to steer myself into a snow bank, and stop my crazy, runaway slide. I started laughing hysterically with tears rolling down my cheeks. I was laughing so hard that I actually peed on myself. This is not an easy thing to hide in tan pants. When Joel finally caught up with me (some hockey player he was!), I was covered in all things wet—tears, snow and pee.

I told him that I couldn't go to the party, all soaking wet. What did he do? He left me there, alone, and went on to the party without me! I ended up escorting my own wet butt, alone in the night, back to the bus stop for a cold, lonely ride home. The lesson I learned that night was not so much not to pee on myself, but to never go out with a man who won't stand by me if I do."

Jennifer, 30

"I WAS OUT WITH THIS GUY WHO WAS 22. (Bad idea!) He took me to a cheap Mexican restaurant, and there were roaches on the wall. I wanted to leave, and he called me 'picky.' So, I suffered through dinner, figuring the date couldn't get any worse. Unfortunately, it did.

After dinner, we went to a bar, and he proceeded to get rip-roaring drunk. He started referring to me in the third person, and just calling me 'this bitch.' I'd had enough, so I got up to leave.

He then asked me, at the top of his lungs in front of a bar full of people, if he was going to be able to 'tap the ass' later. I quickly left, humiliated, and decided I was never again to date any bratty little boys. Tap the ass, indeed!"

Chyna, 25

"I WAS YOUNG AND I MET SOMEONE ONLINE. We were both using fake names, and neither of us had bothered to sufficiently describe ourselves. Big mistake. We still went ahead and had an encounter, but we both ended up being dissatisfied by the whole experience. That's what you get when you don't respect yourself."

Joe, 41

"THE FIRST TIME I HAD SEX was in high school and it was terrible," says Anne. "I faked an orgasm just to get my boyfriend off of me, and I felt horrible about myself for days afterwards. My boyfriend told me we were now bonded in the eyes of God and would have to get married someday! Thank God I had the foresight to break up with the guy!"

Anne, 28

"ONE TIME, MY HIGH SCHOOL boyfriend and I were parked in a new residential area where no one lived yet. I was absolutely naked in the car, and we were fooling around. A cop pulls up, shines his flashlight in the window, and tells me: 'You have to get out of the car.' I asked: 'Can I get dressed first?' He says: 'No, right now.' So, I get out, standing there completely naked in the night. The cop pulls me down to the end of the car and asked if I was being raped! I said: 'No.' He asked if I was sure. I told him I was definitely sure. He then said: 'okay then, don't park here. Move along.' So, I got back in the car, my boyfriend pulled away, and we found somewhere else to park.

But our funniest dating story happened because of my dog. I had a cocker spaniel named 'Pookie' that would eat anything. He was particularly fond of underwear, and anything he could dig out of the bathroom trash. One day, after my boyfriend and I did it at my parents' house, the dog found the condom and ate it right in front of us. We freaked out! My boyfriend followed that dog around for two days, waiting for it to poop it out. He was mortified that my parents would find it in the yard. Since I was an only child, my folks would definitely figure out where that condom came from!

Suzie, 34

*   *   *

THE STORY OF THE TEENIE-WEENIE LITTLE WEENIE

It seems only logical to include "The Story of the Teenie-Weenie Little Weenie" with the tales of dating disasters submitted by our readers. This woeful tale was one of the very first stories ever posted to SexinSiliconValley.com, and came from an in-person interview with one of the authors' friends. The incident happened three years ago, and has been infamous in our social circle ever since.

The "Teenie Weenie" story drove many hits to the web site, and was voted "best story" by visitors to the site. The story also struck a nerve—with both men and women—and accounted for the most reader email, with some people amused by the tale, others offended by it.

Here is the complete, unedited Teenie Weenie story, as it appeared on the web site. As with all the stories, the names used in the story are pen names to protect the identities of the participants involved, both of whom are still working in the Bay Area.

The True Story of Victoria and Dennis
—Better known as *The Story of the Teenie Weenie Little Weenie*

Victoria recounts her most memorable Silicon Valley sex experience with a shy smile and an embarrassed laugh. "My first romantic encounter out here was almost enough to make me pack my things and head back East again," Victoria confesses.

Victoria came out to Silicon Valley four years ago. Like most folks, she was lured out with the offer of a high-paying job, pleasant weather and the appeal of the famed California lifestyle.

"Shortly after I arrived, I started dating this guy Dennis, who worked for a famous film company up in the North Bay.

To be honest, I'm not sure now whether I was charmed by the guy, or infatuated with the connections he had to that film company. Dating him made me feel like I was on the inside track of that movie company. He took me on an inside tours of the different company buildings, and even on a tour of one of the world's most famous special effects houses. It was all very, very exciting. We laughed a lot, enjoyed each other's company, and the relationship was going very well until sex came into the picture.

Dennis had one big shortcoming—literally. There was this issue that came between us. An issue of, uh, physical incompatibility."

Victoria laughs nervously, clearing her throat before continuing.

"Okay, so we'd been dating a couple of months, and at first, we'd kept it at kissing and a bit of groping. Things progressed from there, and one day, at his place, we got so heavy into it, I ended up taking off my pants. He got really excited, and stood up to unbutton his jeans. As he was sliding his pants down over his hips, my gaze naturally strayed to his crotch, eagerly looking to see his bulge. (For women, seeing a guy bulging out his pants is a sign we are doing something right.) But, there didn't seem to be any bulge."

Concerned, Victoria wondered if he wasn't erect, and if she didn't excite Dennis enough. His breathing, his caresses and his words indicated he was aroused, but now looking at him, lying next to her in just his black boxers, it looked as if there was nothing there at all—totally flaccid.

"I started kissing him again, as passionately as I knew how, and he began to slide his underwear off. I stopped kissing him so I could fully watch as he removed his boxers. He removed them really, really slowly, trying to be sexy. My eyes were glued to his crotch. For a brief, horrible moment, I wondered if even perhaps he was a flat-chested woman posing as a man, because there just didn't seem to be anything there. I got truly concerned as to what I would see once those boxers finally came all the way off."

To Victoria's relief, Dennis did actually have a penis, but there was one little problem with it.

"I almost gasped out loud when I saw it. Fully erect, it was no larger than my little pinkie. I take that back, I think my little pinkie is longer than his penis. You'd have to see this one to believe it! I reached out to stroke it, thinking that perhaps it wasn't quite all the way erect, and there still might be more yet to come. But no matter how cleverly I stroked, it didn't get any bigger. That's all there was."

Victoria still optimistically proceeded with the lovemaking, reminding herself that size doesn't matter, and thinking perhaps Dennis was an exceptionally skilled lover.

"Perhaps over the years he had learned to compensate for his size with exceptional skill. I mean, after all, it's what you do with what you have that counts, right? Besides, at that point, we were both fully naked and I'd given all the signs I wanted to make love. I didn't feel I could back out then. What could I say: 'Sorry Dennis, I changed my mind because your penis is so small there is no way this encounter is going to be mutually pleasurable.' At that point, I felt like I had to go all the way. "

All the way didn't turn out to be very far. Dennis lay on top of Victoria, kissing her enthusiastically. Victoria spread her legs, and hoped for the best. Dennis pushed himself downward and put his penis inside of her.

"The only way I knew he had entered me, was by looking down at where our bodies joined. I didn't feel a thing," said Victoria. "I'd hoped I'd feel at least a little something! I wrapped my legs up around him, hoping to take him further into me. I wanted to at least feel something. I really did want this to work between us. That's when it happened. He slipped out. He was so small, he simply slipped out.

I guided him back in, thinking it was just a fluke, and he promptly fell out again. He'd pump a few strokes, fall out, then pump some more. He didn't think this was odd at all. In no time at all, he came, and then fell asleep almost instantly.

I rolled over, and he slid out in a slippery mess, but to add insult to injury, the condom was no longer attached to his now even tinier shriveled little thing. So I had to reach inside myself, and fish out the used condom. I was disgusted, and thought that if he was bigger, maybe he would at least fit properly into a condom!

I just lay there for like ten minutes, staring at his shriveled little thing and resenting it. First of all, the condom incident. Okay, like he could have had the decency to hold on to the condom, pull out and dispose of it before dropping off into dreamland. But, now there was another problem.

Because the condom had slipped off with fresh sperm in it, I now had to contend with the worry that his sperm was now swimming all over my female parts, searching for a nice egg to fertilize.

And, even more than that, I was I completely sexually frustrated from the whole experience. The fact that he slipped out time and time again made me feel wide—totally slutty—and I have never been promiscuous. My previous boyfriend had always commented how tight I felt. Feeling wide and too loose was a new, and most unpleasant, feeling."

Despite the awkward evening, Victoria still tried to make the best of the relationship. Figuring sex wasn't everything, she tried to focus on Dennis' other good qualities.

"Dennis was definitely a nice guy, and will make someone a fine husband someday—someone he is physically and emotionally compatible with—but that someone isn't me."

After six months of dating, Victoria broke up with Dennis.

"I'd tried to make the relationship work, I really did. I even briefly wondered about penile implants. I knew I wanted children someday, and maybe there was some sort of implant that could at least make him big enough so we could fit together long enough to conceive a child. I was willing to be flexible about the whole size thing, but perhaps it was his size that led to his other insecurities.

"It was much more than just the sex thing. He became very clingy and I felt completely suffocated. I no longer had a life of my own. He thought our sex life was great and wanted to make love all the time. For me, it was dreadfully boring and I contemplated stapling reading material to the ceiling so I'd have something to do while he slipped in and out, in and out. After a while, it all just got to be way too much. While I still admired the many good qualities that had made us friends in the first place, I had to end our relationship as lovers. It was just too much to take anymore. I found myself avoiding his phone calls, dreading his visits, and breathing a vast sigh of relief when he went home and I had my apartment to myself again.

I wanted to remain friends, but for him, it was either boyfriend-and-girlfriend, or nothing. If I didn't want to date him, he didn't want anything to do with me.

I sure wish him well. I actually feel sorry for him. In a society that unfairly equates manliness with penis size, poor Dennis has the endowment of a Chihuahua.

I'm betting he hasn't had a lot of sex in his lifetime. He's not someone you'd go back to for seconds. A woman needs to feel somewhat tight and virginal every time she is with her man. With Dennis, I felt as wide as the Grand Canyon."

Chapter Seven

Dating in Silicon Valley—the good, the bad and the ugly

THE GOOD

Survey respondents had wildly mixed opinions on the challenges of dating in the Bay Area. Almost half—47 percent—of survey respondents from out of the area reported that dating in Silicon Valley was more challenging than in other areas, while only 25 percent said it was easier. But the majority of those surveyed claimed the quality of sexual encounters (60 percent) and sex partners (56 percent) was better in the Valley.

Many reported frustrations that tied right into 1999 Census Bureau data which found that Silicon Valley had the largest single-man surplus of any major metropolitan area in the country. According to the Census Bureau, Silicon Valley's lopsided dating ratio surpasses even the traditional man-surplus capital, Anchorage, Alaska. As one respondent put it, "Silicon Valley is a single woman's dating paradise."

Our survey results mirrored the inequality of the sexes; 61 percent of respondents were male, 39 percent female. And while we did receive a fair amount of responses from frustrated men, hundreds of the survey respondents who shared their stories on SexinSiliconValley.com showed another side of the Valley—the wonderful spirit of innovation that made this Valley famous is now being applied to the challenges of dating.

Many survey respondents, male and female, straight and gay, reported ample opportunities for sex and dating in Silicon Valley. Some even went so far as to describe the sexual opportunities here as "the best they've ever had." As one respondent said, "There are so many intelligent, creative 'engineer' types who apply the same type of inventiveness to sex. There are amazing men sitting behind computers thinking about sex all day…hot and ready to go! Ditto for women."

Here are a few of their stories.

*　　　　　*　　　　　*

Mac

Mac is 29 year-old male who works in the Import/Export business. Mac moved to Silicon Valley from the East Coast for "Education. Family. Promise."

Mac describes himself as single and swinging, having had eight dates in the past month and more than ten sexual encounters. He finds both the quality, and the availability, of sex partners to be better here than in other areas.

Mac makes good use of the Internet, and has found several dating partners through online chat rooms and bulletin boards. His last sexual encounter ranked a nine out of 10 and was with a casual friend. Mac describes the encounter as follows: "Lighting…timing, the general vigor and passion that was involved…very primal, but at the same time, very civilized."

Mac enjoys sex in unusual places, and the list includes "a vineyard, a dressing room, a plane bathroom, a wedding ceremony, and," he adds, "the list goes on."

The vineyard incident was the most recent. "We went wine tasting and got inspired to take a bit of a self-guided tour. Love was in the air. There was a wedding rehearsal going on, and it made us both feel a bit amorous.

We grabbed flutes of champagne, and sneaked around to the top of this hill, where we could see everything that was going on.

It started to rain and we were both aroused by the idea of doing it right there in the vineyard, with the light rain misting down on us.

We moved underneath a tree, out of eyeshot (or so we thought, but you never know, and that thought made it even more exciting!).

I unzipped my pants and tugged her pants and panties down around her knees. I lifted her up, and pumped into her upright, holding her against the tree.

It took me no time at all to come in that position, and I made sure she had her enjoyment too, by reaching my fingers between her legs and rubbing her just right as I pumped into her. I mean, what kind of guy would I be if I didn't take care of her pleasure along with my own?

After we both came, and tugged our clothes back on our damp bodies, we gulped down out champagne, then threw the flutes behind us with a crash. We meandered back to the car feeling mischievous and crazy."

When asked what his ideal sexual encounter would be, Mac says dreamily: "hot group sex."

William

William, age 28, moved to Silicon Valley from New York. He came to the Bay Area out of a "desire for a more liberal, slightly freaky, less money/yuppie driven culture than the East Coast."

William works in the wine industry, and in the almost five years he's been in the Bay Area, he's found dating easier compared to other areas.

William is currently in a committed relationship, but during his single days, he found locating sexual partners much easier than on the East Coast. "The area still has a liberal underbelly, and sex is available, if you just know where to look," says William.

"The most liberal women I have ever met have all been out here in the Bay Area. Women (or at least the ones I've been with out here), seem more willing to try different things. They more easily express what they want out of a sexual relationship," he says.

He's also found other advantages to being in the Bay Area: "It's much easier to come by a 'friends with benefits' relationship here than anywhere else."

William and his girlfriend enjoy sex together several times a week. William thoughtfully ponders his most recent lovemaking session: "When you are with someone for an extended period of time, sex seems to go through highs and lows. Currently, my partner and I are in one of our high times. Today was definitely a peak, starting from first thing in the morning.

We had a playful sexual romp in bed as soon as we awoke. We were both just ready. Afterwards, we showered together, and enjoyed a substantial homemade brunch. Full and sated, we spent the day running around the city. Later, as we were relaxing in the living room, it occurred to me I hadn't gone down on my girlfriend for some time. I could feel myself getting hard just thinking about it. I moved over to her on my knees, and she knew right away what was coming. I stayed on my knees, pleasuring her with my tongue, as she sat with her legs spread-eagled on the edge of the couch. We both love that position! After I'd brought her to orgasm using my tongue, I stood up, and she slowly undressed me. Her tongue moved down my body until she reached my groin and took me into her mouth. After I was about as full, hard and throbbing as I could possibly get, we moved to the floor to complete the act.

In thinking about what made today's sex so great, I think it was a combination of factors all working together. Some of it was the spontaneity—from being fully clothed in our living room—to being naked with me licking her in a matter of moments. Some was the visual—it was light, middle of the day, and she could watch me pleasing her, just as I could later watch her sucking me.

But there was more. There was the creativity of it all, the hotness of how we do it. I used the windowsill, the entertainment center and the coffee table for balance as we pleasured ourselves in many different positions before finally climaxing.

Then there was the sound of it all. Not just our bodies slapping together with that sound only sex can make, it was how vocal my girl-friend became. She moaned very loudly as we were finishing, and this made me come at the same time. Such a turn on to know that those noises are happening because you are doing something right! And, of course, it's always a feeling of pride and satisfaction when you manage to come at the same time. Just makes you feel very in sync with the other person."

When asked about his most unusual sexual encounter, William thinks fondly back to a dressing room at the local mall. "My girlfriend at the time starting giving me head while I was trying on pants," William remembers, "Shortly thereafter, she was riding me on the bench, facing away from me, both of us watching ourselves in the mirror. Mmmmmm.... what a memory!"

William's best sex ever was with an anonymous partner he met through an online encounter.

"We had cyber and phone sex," says William, "and then we met the next day, ostensibly for lunch. Lunch didn't last long! We quickly retreated to my place, where we did just about everything. I would describe her approach as more like a guy—she liked it all, and the dirtier the better! She gave me head in front of the mirror and I shot all over her face. We did anal in the shower and did several positions while watching porn. It was amazing!"

When asked what his ideal sexual encounter would be, William says: "Another one just like the anonymous encounter. The anonymity is such a turn on!"

Jennifer

Jennifer is a 30 year-old Marketing Manager, originally from Tennessee and Boston. She moved out here five years ago "for a boy. He got a job with Sun Microsystems and it seemed pretty harmless to leave everything behind and follow him out here with his new job."

The two have since married and are happily settled into the life of a Silicon Valley couple. "Though I am married, when I first moved out here as a single woman, I was continually hit on by guys. None were particularly appealing, though. I've been perfectly content sticking by the man I have."

Jennifer and her husband enjoy sex at least once or twice a week, and the most recent time rated a "six" due to some "pet complications":

"We were at a friend's house as guests for the night. They have a very furry cat to whom my husband was extremely allergic. Oral sex and sneezing do not go well together."

When talking about the more passionate side of their relationship, Jennifer describes her husband's amazing linguistic abilities:

"I love dirty talk," confides Jennifer. "When I first met the man who would later become my husband, we held off a number of months before having sex. During that long period, he would say things to me that I hadn't even heard in porn films.

He could make me orgasm without ever touching me. I would orgasm just from his dirty talk. Phone sex became an exciting new frontier for me! He would say: 'Come on, Jen. Come on,' with such intensity.

During that same time, I started listening to a band called B-Tribe which has a song wherein the singer says 'Come on' in the same fashion. I would sit at work listening to that CD over and over, getting excited just from hearing those two words!

Since we've been married now for a number of years, the dirty talk doesn't surface very often, but when it does…I'm ready to go in SECONDS.

I've since learned that there is a certain 'fetish' out there called (I think) 'autolalia' that is simply dirty talk. I plan on doing some research into that field of study…"

Jennifer has never tried cybersex, but does shyly admit: "Internet porn does play a role in our sex lives. There is some HOT stuff available online!"

Jennifer's most unusual sexual encounter occurred in a ski gondola, swinging high above snowy mountain peaks.

"My boyfriend at the time worked at Keystone resort in Colorado. We were going up to a bar at the top of the mountain—there were many people in line for the gondola. He knew the guy who was letting people into the cars and convinced him with a wink and a nudge to let us go up alone.

Apparently, my boyfriend had ridden the gondola a few times before and had timed the ride. He knew that we had eight minutes and 20 seconds to the top of the mountain.

Before the doors even closed, he was unzipping his pants. He was fully-erect, throbbing, and ready to go. We had the ultimate quickie—I sat on his lap nearly fully-clothed while the gondola swung precariously hundreds of feet over the snow fields.

It was a beautiful sight to look down upon, but give me eight minutes and 20 seconds of foreplay over that ANY day. I'm sure it was a huge turn-on for him, but it didn't do much for me. Pump, pump, pump, done. Yeah, like that does anything to arouse a woman in all the right places."

When asked about her best sexual experience, Jennifer thinks fondly back to a very talented boy she dated years ago. "I had a boyfriend for a very little while—about four weeks right after I got out of college—who could do the most amazing things with his hands. I didn't even need oral from this man—his mouth wasn't nearly as good as his hands. He could put his hands in my pants and have me coming for hours—great orgasms that were as intense as I had ever had with my college boyfriend.

I would beg him to get a mirror so I could see what he was doing down there, but he refused. I asked him to describe it, but he was too shy. This is a man who would run the water in the sink in the bathroom at full force while he was peeing so I wouldn't hear him urinate. Yes, he was very odd.

But, he looked good, and... those HANDS!

It's been almost ten years since I saw him last, and our final parting was not a good one. (His girlfriend showed up—he had forgotten to mention that he had one of those!)

But, I will never forget the feeling of those hands, and wonder what he was doing down there that was so incredibly magic. Oftentimes, I touch myself, trying to recapture the feelings he evoked, but thus far, I've never quite recaptured that same feeling. I might never know. Damn!"

Brett

Brett is a 27 year-old Communications Manager, originally from New York. Brett knew since he was 15 that he wanted to live and work in the Bay Area. He is currently single, and describes his single status as "swinging." He finds the availability and quality of sex partners here to be better than in his native New York.

Brett's last sexual encounter was with a casual dating partner. "The most exciting thing was that my partner shaved her genitalia," Brett says, "It was a first for me, and being the cunnilingus enthusiast I am, I found it very stimulating."

The most unusual place Brett's had sex was "in a bed in a small room with five other people asleep around us. It was just one of those things. It was more of a lack of choice, than making one."

Brett's best sexual encounter was with a friend that Brett describes as "an incredibly fit, very attractive former cheerleader."

Brett tells the story of their hot, satisfying encounter: "We left a bar together at closing. In the middle of the parking lot (the location was somewhat isolated), we made out as it started to rain. I lifted her up onto the trunk of her car and gave her oral pleasure until she climaxed. Between the rain and her orgasm, she was very wet indeed!"

Jon

Jon is a 32 year-old Lab Technician, originally from Mission Viejo, California. Jon gives the Silicon Valley dating scene high marks. He ranks dating here as easier than other areas, opportunities for sex as more readily available, and the quality of sex partners as better than other areas.

"There are lot of like-minded people in this area," says Jon. "It makes it much easier to find dates."

Compared to other areas, Jon finds people in the Bay Area more straight forward. "There is less pretext here," says Jon. "People know what they want. This area is conducive to instant gratification, whether it's sexual or otherwise."

Jon is a big fan of cybersex. "It is easy, cheap and fun—the ultimate safe sex experience!"

Jon enjoys sex over 10 times a month with his significant other, and ranks his last sexual encounter as an eight out of 10. "It was really hot," says Jon. "Everything was done by non-verbal communication. No words were necessary. Just lots of eye contact and knowing just how to please each other. I felt really connected with her!"

The most unusual place Jon's enjoyed sex is outside the Mitchell Brothers O' Farrell Theater. "A woman took me there for my birthday," remembers Jon. "As we were making our way back to her car after the show, it just happened. I went to open her door, and slid my hand up her skirt. She didn't object, so I kissed her, a real deep, open-mouth kind of kiss. She returned the kiss just as I lifted her up onto the hood of the car and pulled her panties to one side. I unzipped my fly, and whipped myself out. I was so hard and ready! I just slipped in, right then and there, with my pants still on and people walking by. We didn't even care. We climaxed right there on her car hood!"

When asked about his best sex ever, Jon remembers his earliest sexual experiences. "The best ever was the second time I had sex. The first time was rushed, and I just wanted to get it over with so I could get past being a virgin. The second time was so different—so fluid and beautiful. I was with my girlfriend in a small cabin in Carmel. I didn't even know we were going to do it—which was part of what made it so cool! We went from one phase to another, and I literally melted into her the moment I slid myself into her."

When asked if he had any other comments, Jon says: "Shhhhhh! I'll let you in on a little secret. I like to have cybersex as a woman. I go into lesbian chat rooms, and get women off, posing as a woman myself. It's awesome!"

Mamie

Mamie is a 25 year-old Administrative Assistant from Kansas. When asked why she came to the Bay Area, Mamie answered: "Bright Lights, Big City."

Mamie has been in the Bay Area for three years, and is currently single. She finds dating here easier than in her native Kansas. She also finds the sexual partners to be of better quality.

The last time she had sex was "with a co-worker. What was good about it? Well, it wasn't weird afterwards at work. Not for long, anyway. Just casual. No strings attached. You couldn't do that in Kansas.

What was bad about it? It was casual. I've heard, but I'm not sure, that sex gets better after several times with the same partner. I'm not that experienced and haven't really met anyone who is looking for long-term, or even medium-range commitment. So, all the sex I've had has been casual and short-term. I'm looking forward to meeting someone whom I can really open up to and explore sexually, and I'm looking forward to them exploring me."

When comparing the Bay Area to other areas she has lived, Mamie comments: "I've lived in Kansas and in Atlanta, and sex there is something you only talk about in whispers and do in the dark. Here, sex is not such a taboo subject. You can talk about it, and about getting it, without seeming scared of it. It seems more fun, without being slutty.

While there is still the stigma of a being a slut if a GIRL sleeps around too much, it is not as bad as other places I have lived. Of course, the rules are totally different for guys. Almost universally, a guy who sleeps around a lot is considered a stud.

There are other advantages to being single here. People stay single here longer than in other parts of the country. No one expects a 30 year-old single person to not have ever played around.

In Kansas, if you are 30 and have never been married, you would be considered an old maid who is over the hill, and kind of pathetic. Not here. 30 year-olds are considered as being in their prime here."

When asked about the most unusual place she's had sex, Mamie admits: "Well, it wasn't actually penetration, but I did do some exhibitionist playing around at a sex club.

I was a virgin, at a sex club one crazy night. There was a guy there who I thought was good looking.

It didn't take much conversation before we were making out and touching each other in places it feels good to be touched.

I still find it hard to believe I did it as the people walking around the club would stop to watch us. But, I just didn't care. We never actually had sex, but we rubbed and tantalized through our underwear, and at one point, we both had our shirts off!"

Mary Jane

Mary Jane moved here from Oregon a year ago "for the perfect man," who is now her fiancé. Mary Jane tells the story of how they met: "I had given up on dating in my home state of Oregon. So I started checking out the Internet personals. I wasn't seriously looking for a boyfriend, just browsing to see what was out there. I came upon an ad that really caught my eye, so I sent the guy a message.

We began emailing each other, and then a week later we moved on to online instant messaging. Soon, he wanted my phone number because he had to hear 'the voice behind the amazing personality.' I was a little wary, so I told him that if he gave me his phone number, I would call him. That night, I called him, and from that moment on, we talked every night. I flew down here to meet him face-to-face on January 7th of 2000 and we've been together, in love, ever since."

Mary Jane and her fiancé enjoy a rich, active sex life. "Sex between us is always wonderful," says Mary Jane, "Our last encounter, I'd rate a nine out of 10 because there is always room for improvement. Nothing is absolutely perfect. With the two of us, it's more about the foreplay than the actual act. We love to rub each others' bodies and kiss and tease so much that when he actually penetrates me, it's like an explosion for both of us.

Plus, there's some form of oral in every session we have. We just have an extremely gratifying sex life together. It's not like anything I've experienced before. We're very happy to be engaged and planning our lives together."

They are also a very sexual couple. "We have sex EVERY day." reports Mary Jane, "Sometimes, we have to have it more than once a day. On average, I would say that we have sex about 30-36 times a month. On weekends, sometimes we do it more than twice a day. Even during my monthly 'time,' my boyfriend knows it's blowjob week. I refuse to let him go unsatisfied just because a part of me is under construction."

With such frequent lovemaking, the couple works hard to keep their sex life fresh and exciting. "My guy really has what it takes. He takes complete control of pleasuring me before he even thinks about himself. He's the most wonderful lover, and tells me I'm also very talented in the bedroom. We're always coming up with some new position."

New locales and a spirit of adventure also help keep them entertained. "Once we did it in the car, on the way home from his parents house. He was driving and I took off my seatbelt, unzipped his pants and went down. He was driving the whole time, although he did need to pull over for the finale.

Another time, we were on the hood of my car while it was raining. It was nighttime and it was misting, just enough to get you a little wet. We pulled over into an out of the way area, and I leaned up and over the hood of my car.

He got behind me, tore off my panties, and stuck his very erect penis into me. He penetrated me from behind, gliding in and out, faster and faster, while I held on to the rain soaked hood. I was so excited because anyone could have driven up and seen us!"

Their most memorable encounter took place in a hotel. "He had just gotten out of the shower. I was standing in front of the mirror, in a dress. He came up behind me, naked and still a bit damp, and start kissing the back of my neck and rubbing me. He then pulled down my panties and pulled them off. He sat me up on the counter, and spread my legs apart so he could see everything.

He was so intense with passion that I was already getting flushed. He started kissing me, and then he entered me—fast and furious and passionate. We were watching ourselves in the mirror, and getting more turned on. There's been so many good times between us, it's hard to pick just one time, but if I had to pick, THAT was the best sex I ever had. Every other time since then would tie for second best."

When asked what he ideal sexual encounter would be, Mary Jane answers: "I don't know that I can actually describe my ideal sexual encounter. My boyfriend has pretty much made all my fantasies come true. I get everything that I want in the bedroom. So, my ideal sexual encounter is ANYWHERE and ANYTHING with him."

Mary Jane knows she is very fortunate to enjoy such a fulfilling sex life, and feels compassion for her less fortunate sisters in the Valley. But she also believes women are partly to blame. "For most of the women around here, it's all about how much money a man makes, or what kind of car he drives. I find that to be disgusting! Whatever happened to judging someone by charm and personality? Many of the men I know have it, but it's not accompanied by a big bankroll and a BMW to match, so women don't give them a second glance.

The women are the ones who are missing out by being such gold-diggers. They aren't getting any sex because they refuse to consider dating a guy who drives a Honda hatchback. Hey ladies, I have news for you. Those are often times the guys who are most talented in the bedroom! Men who drive normal cars aren't the ones overcompensating to make up for their lack of skill or physical endowment!

Love is not about how big a guy's paycheck is. It's about what's in his heart, and once a girl has a guy's heart, there is no limit to what the two of them can do in the bedroom. Or, any other room for that matter…"

For some women, Silicon Valley is truly a single woman's dating paradise. They find the quality and availability of sexual partners to be superior to other areas, with more than enough opportunities to keep a single woman very happy and occupied. Here are the stories of ladies who are enjoying stellar sex in the Bay Area…

Joy

Joy is a 34 year-old Finance Director, originally from Arizona. Joy came to Silicon Valley seven years ago for a job. She is unmarried, but currently in a committed relationship.

She has found dating in Silicon Valley easier than other areas. "People are more friendly and approachable here," says Joy. "Mostly the common demographics makes it possible—majority of people I come into contact with are 25-40, professional, college-degreed, etc."

She finds the quality, and availability of sexual partners to be better than other areas. "More men than woman, do the math! Being single, female, fairly attractive, fit…Hey, it's way too easy to get laid here."

Joy also enjoys the sensitive sides of the men she has met here. "Men here are more fragile, open up emotionally easier, and you can connect with them better. It takes a soft voice and a soft touch to completely melt away any feigned machismo or toughness in just a few minutes… more intelligent people also SEEM to have deeper emotions, issues—things they're personally wrestling with but would love to share with the right person that can listen."

She provides positive feedback on the performance of her sexual partners: "They are more experienced here, more feedback how-am-I-doing oriented."

Joy's last sexual encounter rated an impressive 10 out of 10.

When asked if she's tried cybersex, Joy answered: "No need when the real thing is abundant!"

Rory

Rory is a 54 year-old female Technical/Applications/Web Designer. Originally from Washington, DC, Rory describes her single status as "single and swinging." Rory has enjoyed more than 10 dates in the past month, and finds dating in Silicon Valley much easier than other areas.

"The dates are out there ladies," says Rory, "You just have to know how to find and entice the men!"

She has enjoyed sex more than 10 times in the past month, and comments: "The sex partners in Silicon Valley are ab-so-lut-e-ly incredible!"

Rory is a big fan both of online dating and cybersex. Rory comments on online dating: "By meeting your dates online before you meet them in person, you can establish parameters and expectations."

Rory's experiences with cybersex have been very positive: "With the right partner, it is fan-tas-tic!" Rory's cybersex activities also have led to successful in-person meetings. "Meeting my cybersex partner in person was even better than I imagined! Great connection. We really got to know each other before we met. No secrets. I could tell this man my innermost thoughts, desires, wishes and fantasies. We might have spent years learning as much about each other if we'd met some other way."

The most unusual place Rory has enjoyed sex is "on the way home from Hawaii. United First Class, in the restroom. Use your imagination."

Rory's only experienced one dating disaster after meeting someone online. "I set up a date with a guy who called himself 'TooTall.' He wasn't!

He lied about both his height and his age. In addition, he was a pervert! Luckily, we met during broad daylight in a very public place, and I was able to extricate myself from the situation."

She offers these final comments: "If women are sitting around saying men are hard to find… you better believe the men are doing the same thing. Take control of your destiny!!! Try Internet dating! I feel like a kid again…a kid in a candy store! I have met the nicest, kindest, sexiest men in the last 60 days."

THE BAD

Not surprisingly, more men (53 percent) than women (37 percent) believe dating in Silicon Valley is more difficult than in other areas. It's that dreaded single-man surplus. According to the 1999 Census Bureau data, there were 5,372 more single men than women aged 20 to 45 in Santa Clara County, the heart of Silicon Valley. Other large metropolitan areas typically have single-men deficits. Many men in the Valley are frustrated, angry and losing hope.

But dating difficulties aren't just limited to men. Several of our female interviewees described dating disasters and disappointments as they navigated the challenging Valley social scene. As one female survey respondent said, "There are too many hungry men. They're desperate for women, and will take whatever they can get. And that just ain't sexy."

Add to that the 16-hour days spent building the next new thing, the faltering economy, the traffic congestion and the high cost of living and, well, it's bad all around.

*   *   *

Peter

Peter, 27, is a student who has lived in Silicon Valley "almost all my life." He is single and alone, and had just one date in recent months. He ranks Silicon Valley as being "more difficult to get dates" when compared to other areas.

"Women are less friendly here, than in say, San Francisco," says Peter. "There are so many men here, that women don't feel they have to be nice or smart or interesting."

When asked when was the last time he had sex, Peter replied: "What's sex? My last sexual encounter involved my hand, which made me content, but not fulfilled."

His biggest dating disaster was with a woman "suffering from pot-induced a-motivational syndrome." He describes her as large, "but paradoxically, without any curves. Her shoulders were broad, but her hips were narrower than mine. She also had quite a gut. And no, I did not ask her out on a second date!"

Maggie

Maggie, 48, moved to the Bay Area 10 years ago for a job. She is divorced, a student, and finding the dating scene to be challenging.

"I'm currently living in Sunnyvale, and everyone drives, and only goes out to clubs. There's less foot traffic here than in the city, and less intimacy than in smaller towns. There seems to be more 'hit and run' sex here. People seem to view other people as commodities. They're in permanent 'buy' mode."

When asked if she's had cybersex, Maggie says: "What's the point? I can masturbate alone without dragging anyone else into it."

Cathy

Cathy is a student in her early 20's, pursuing a degree in Art. Originally from New England, she has been in the Bay Area less than a year. Cathy finds the dating scene more challenging than back East: "Most of the guys I've met—even the straight ones—are so artificial. They are all about clothes and their damn cell phones. I've pretty much given up any hopes of meeting any real guys out here. But I'm only here until I graduate, so I've settled for casual sex instead. Thank God for craigslist! That's one thing you won't find in a small New Hampshire town."

Cathy says meeting men online takes some getting used to. "First four times it was kind of weird, but you get used to it!"

There's a very important sexual milestone that Cathy has yet to achieve. She describes her dilemma: "The guy I'm dating is seven years older than me, and has lots of stamina. It takes him a long time to finally get off, which leaves me tired and sore, and always unfulfilled. I have yet to have an orgasm—ever."

Recently, Cathy and her boyfriend participating in an "aural" peeping Tom session: "We were having sex in my boyfriend's dorm room," said Cathy, "and the walls were so thin that we could hear a threesome going on next door. The noises were a real turn-on! My boyfriend and I really started getting into it, making quite a bit of sex noises of our own. Pretty soon, we hear the single guy in the room to the right of us, getting off on the noises we were making! We just kept going right at it, with all those sex noises surrounding us until my boyfriend climaxed. Funny enough, later on, our friends tell us they had come by to get us for dinner, but when they heard all the noise going on, they just sat down outside the door and listened!"

When asked to describe her ideal sexual experience, Cathy says: "One in which I finally have an orgasm! I don't care where it is!"

Rob

Rob is a 28 year old System Administrator who moved to Silicon Valley from Chicago for "work, baby…work." He finds dating here more challenging than other areas he's lived including Chicago, Vegas and South Beach, and finds both the quality and availability of sex partners are worse.

"Girls are much less attractive here," says Rob, "But, then again, it is harder to fall victim to the 'single Mom syndrome.'"

Despite the challenges, Rob still seems to be doing well on the sex front. When asked about the most unusual place he's had sex, Rob answers: "In the Bay Area? BART. But, if handjobs count, it was at PacBell Park. When asked for the details of some of his unusual sexual encounters, Rob elaborates: "The sex on the BART kinda blew (not literally). But, then again, I didn't like the girl I was with.

The handjob at PacBell Park, on the other hand, was totally unexpected, so that made it that much better. I couldn't really conceal my uh…enthusiasm and I ruined a perfectly good t-shirt. But, there was a downside. I had gotten the tickets through my aunt, who has season tickets. The people behind us asked where she and my uncle were. I introduced myself and my girlfriend, and we actually got along, until my girlfriend started getting tipsy, and bored, unzipped my pants and fondled me until I shot all over myself. I guess we weren't overly discreet, because sad to say, I haven't been offered seats since."

Kevin

Kevin, late 20s, moved here from southern California. "I've found that the 'scene' up here isn't much different than it is in southern California. Don't get me wrong. I love the Bay Area. It has a totally different vibe, and as a whole, it's not as materialistic and much more-open minded.

However, the singles scene is very much the same. I think it's probably due to the places that we go to meet people. People always tell me: 'you're never going to meet anyone in a bar.' My response is 'where the hell am I supposed to meet anyone.'

People, and unfortunately, predominantly women go out to be seen and get an ego-boost. They don't really want to meet anyone. They want to look good and even shoot a look or two at a guy to see if he'll approach her. Then, she just sends him on his way.

I think dating, being single, and meeting women is probably difficult everywhere. About two months ago, I went to a bar and met an attractive girl. She was by herself, obviously waiting for friends, but didn't look comfortable. I made a simple joke, introduced myself, and told her she could chill with my circle of friends until her friends showed up. I asked her a couple of questions to keep the conversation going, and she asked me if I had a job. I said: 'That's interesting. I came up here for work, but just got laid off last Monday.' Her response? She said: 'Well, nice meeting you," and walked off."

In lamenting the woes of trying to date in the Valley, many women spoke of Silicon Valley men being afraid to approach women, afraid to even say hello, much less ask a woman out on a date. Some attributed this to the high number of engineers in the area, and the natural tendency of many engineers to be shy, withdrawn types. Others attributed this to lack of social experiences in college, due to male-dominated Engineering classes (not enough interaction with women). Still, others felt the long hours worked by Valley engineers didn't allow them enough opportunities to work on their social and dating skills.

Tara

Tara is a 35 year-old designer, originally from Orange County. She came to the Bay Area two years ago for work. She is currently single.

She finds dating here easier than other areas, and ranks the area as having a greater availability of sexual partners than her native Orange County, CA. "But," says Tara, "I only have sex if I'm involved in a relationship."

Tara has tried cybersex, and describes it as "Fun—in a raunchy way."

Tara's most unusual sexual encounter occurred close to sea: "It was on a table in the dining room a yacht club. It was 3:00 a.m., the halyards were slapping against the main, and moonlight was dancing on the water…"

Tara has a definitive romantic side. Her best sex ever was: "with a guy I was really in love with, in front of the fireplace. It was the way he looked at me."

Tara describes her ideal sexual encounter: "Being completely in love and at ease with each other's bodies, in a nice romantic setting…"

When asked if she had any other comments, Tara asked: "Why are Silicon Valley men so afraid to approach women? They will stare at you all night long and then leave. If you approach them, they become swaggering ego-maniacs and instantly lose every ounce of charm! Say hello, it won't kill you."

*   *   *

THE UGLY

"Stephen" submitted his story in its entirety via email. His story was so amusing that we decided to give him his own section within this chapter. While we don't necessarily agree with Stephen's judgmental views of women, we are looking to present a balanced viewpoint of dating in the Bay Area, and Stephen is entitled to his opinion. Stephen's story, entitled "Butterface" was featured on SexinSiliconValley.com and quickly became a hit with readers. So, now that you have read about the good and the bad, it's time to read about the ugly.

The Story of Stephen Y
—AKA *Butterface*

"After returning to the Bay Area two years ago, I took a job at a decent e-commerce start-up. I was lured by the good pay, stock options, and good funding of the company.

Having lived in the Bay Area, I knew the opportunity to meet hot young women would not match San Diego in terms of numbers. But, I thought there had to be at least one golden nugget in the Valley, and I was determined to find it.

At my new job, I ended up working with geeky engineers, mostly guys from various international countries. And the women? The women I worked with looked like they had fallen out of the ugly tree and hit every branch on the way down.

The only way I was meeting good looking women was at this restaurant in Palo Alto I would frequent. I'd eat alone at the bar three to four times a week, hoping to meet that golden nugget.

I had a decent criteria that I would go by: no married women, no kids, divorced was okay, had to be intelligent, and had to be hot with either big tits or rocking tight body and a pretty face.

For a while, I was meeting one to three girls a night, on different levels of the scale. But, many of them turned out to be 'butterfaces.' Everything was hot—body, tits, ass—but their faces! Yuck!

Occasionally, I would meet a nine or a 10, but it always ended up being the same story—still married, trying to get divorced, just wanted a friend, or a shoulder to cry on. And some, were just plain dumb.

So, I decided, what the heck, I am going to downgrade my expectations to the six-seven level, and go for the 'butterfaces.' I figured they'd be real easy for me to get.

Sure enough, the second night after I lowered my expectations, I met the perfect 'butterface.' She was a Vice-President of a large chip manufacturing company in San Jose. She had huge tits, nice ass, teeny waist, perfect sandy blonde hair, 32 years-old, single—and a total butterface.

She had a gigantic nose that could be seen when viewing her from behind at about 45 degrees to either side. She reminded me of the colorful Hornbills I had once seen in Southeast Asia. The ears were a sight to see, as they could hold back large quantities of hair without using a clip—akin to the satellite dish on the hill at Stanford University.

But the body! I could just imagine plunging into her body as I looked at her skimpy little dress, great set of tits, tanned legs and expensive shoes.

Now, the difficult part. How do I quickly get her out of this popular downtown Palo Alto restaurant, and into bed, without being seen by people I know?

I ordered two shots of the finest tequila they had. We each downed the shots. I hate hard liquor and almost puked. Most unfortunately, the first shot didn't seem to have much effect on butterface.

'Two more shots, please,' I quickly asked the waiter.

We downed the tequila, and the second shot worked like a charm. She'd already had quite a bit of wine, and the tequila treatment was kicking into overdrive. It was time to expedite things.

'Why don't we head back to my place and watch a DVD? I just got the first season of *Sex in the City* from Amazon.com,' I suggested.

Perfect! She loved the idea, and offers to drive. Her car turned out to be a brand new black Jag convertible, with the top down! She wanted to go the long way back to my place and decides to drive down University Avenue.

I slithered really low into the seat to avoid being seen, but it was too late. Two buddies from college saw me while we were stopped at the light.

"Hey Stephen!" they called out. Then, I saw them both look at each other, thinking what the %$#@! is he doing with that butterface? I knew that later I'm going to get a lot of grief for this, but I was committed to going all the way with her.

She started rubbing my leg on the way home, and was talking about how she hadn't been with a nice guy in a long time.

I responded to her while staring at her tits, or her tanned ever-so-slight catfish belly that exposed her belly button ring. She didn't seem to mind as I'm betting she knew the 80/20 rule—80% of her body's mass was beyond perfect, the other 20% looked like a biotech company's botched experiments with human genomes.

We got back to my place in Menlo Park, and I pour some Merlot, dim the lights, and start to load the DVD player.

To my surprise, she reached through my legs from behind and squeezed my nuts. I played it cool, and continued to load the disc, like this happened all the time.

But, when I turned around, she was standing there half-naked, wearing only a bright-red G-string, with the hottest fake boobs and great tan lines. She was holding a tube of Astroglide in her left hand, and smiling with her ever present snaggletooth (argh!).

We immediately started to make out, and I found it difficult to kiss her. Not only because she was ugly, but her nose made it difficult to maneuver my head sideways to gain clearance to her mouth.

Needless to say, the kissing ended in about a minute.

I jumped into my birthday suit, and immediately started to maneuver myself down to her golden triangle.

I slipped the G-string aside, and began licking the sweetest box I had ever tasted. The pubic hairs were trimmed to perfection. The box was as tight as could be, and she began moaning like there was no tomorrow.

Reciprocating the favor, she guided me to the couch, and started to swallow my rod whole. I couldn't believe it—this butterface turned out to be the best lay I'd had since college.

I decide it was time for the full banana boat ride, and I turn her hot body around. I slipped on the condom, and did her from behind. What a fantastic lay! I was just pounding into her love muffin.

We were going at it for a good 20 minutes, when she paused and reached for her purse. She quickly pulled out a shiny metal dildo. She asked me to lube it up and stick it into her behind while I am pounding her.

I thought, 'This is some weird shit,' as I hadn't even seen a dildo in person before. But, what the heck?

I leaned back, still continuing the motion, and slid the dildo up her ass. I felt like a freaking porn star—poking her with two things! She climaxed, yelled, and started biting and dribbling on the nice silk pillow on my couch. I pulled out of her, whipped off the rubber sprayed my seed all over her back and hair.

I never did see her again. It was such a weird experience to have a women so into strange sex with toys on a first date. I knew then that I had to cut bait. I never saw her again."

*   *   *

MIXED REVIEWS

Silicon Valley. The name alone conjures images of tech wizards, instant millionaires, 25 year-old CEOs and money, money, money. Even with a looming recession, the Valley still claims the highest per-capita income in the nation. And while the Internet bust has tarnished its allure a bit, Silicon Valley still draws the best and brightest from other states and around the world.

For those of us that live, work and date here, the Valley is an amazing place; it is still the Valley of the heart's delight, as it was called before the silicon invasion. We are blessed with sunshine 320 days a year. Unemployment is (usually) lower than the national average. We have an abundance of choice; from skiing in Tahoe to surfing in Santa Cruz, the Bay Area is a single person's playground. So what's not to like?

Well…for starters, those instant millionaires drove up the cost of housing, making the Bay Area one of the most expensive places to live in the country. Most of our high incomes go towards housing. Like the joke says, "Only in the Bay Area can you make $100,000 a year and still not be able to afford an apartment!" If you are single, chances are you have a roommate…or three. And whomever you're dating has one, too, so privacy is not easy to come by.

As for those millionaires—they earned that money by toiling long into the night, every night, along with the rest of us. All of which makes dating a challenge, to say the least. But as these survey respondents have found, good sex – even great sex – is possible, with a little imagination.

*   *   *

Faith

Faith is a 33 year-old designer, originally from northern California. Faith has tried cybersex, but "only as a joke."

Her last sexual encounter occurred "in the past year, with a casual partner." The sex was very good, rating a nine out of 10.

Faith describes their encounter: "There was so much good about it. The boy was so yummy, and smelled wonderful. He paid attention to me—what I wanted, and how I responded. He could stay hard for a very long time. He played with my kitty for a very long time with his mouth, and he responded to my requests with zest!

I love this conversation we had one night during doggy-style sex. I think about it often...I watched him do me doggy-style in a mirror. He was standing up. His right hand was on my butt and his thumb rubbed my b-hole. He had that look on this face. He was so into this.

I asked him: 'You really like coming this way, huh?'

He said, as he lightly touched each spot he would refer to, 'I like coming this way with YOU. I like to see your wrinkled brow, your dimple, your sculpted back...'

The only bad part about the sex that night was it was late. Way too late. We didn't have enough time to spend enjoying each other's bodies. There is so much about this guy to enjoy, so I hate it when we are rushed. He'll talk and share lots, so it's always a sexual conversation too. I wish I could have more sex with that yummy boy, but he is moving out of the area (sigh)."

When asked about the most unusual place she's had sex, Faith thinks back fondly to a Christmas party at the Santa Clara Convention Center.

"The party was ending," remembers Faith, "and I saw this out-of-the-way bathroom. I guided my date in there, and we went into a stall. I put my back against the wall and held onto the stall while he positioned himself below me. I lowered myself onto him, and then moved myself up and down, using only my arm strength and one leg on the floor. It was a most memorable Christmas party!

I've had sex in cars, on top of the cars, in the back of cars, given blowjobs while kneeling in the backup of a pickup—all the high school stuff that bored teenagers do in small towns!"

While Faith has enjoyed some good sexual encounters, her view of dating in Silicon Valley is surprisingly pessimistic: "I can't believe there's anyone getting laid in the Valley," says Faith. "Dating isn't easy here. There are too many hungry men. It wouldn't matter what you acted like, or if you weren't really attractive. The men are desperate for women, and will take whatever they can get. That just ain't sexy—and I'm all about sexy.

The men are way too geeky, and can't dress or bathe it seems. Truth be told, there are some very unattractive men in Silicon Valley. San Francisco has better looking men, but the really hot boys are usually gay. It's so frustrating!

I sometimes go to bars to meet people, but being a little older than many bar hoppers, when I meet a cute boy, he often turns out to be too young to date. God, I don't want to train another man how to lick my kitty. I want him to come already loaded with his own toolbox. Bring me the MEN."

Jean

Jean is a 28 year-old attorney, originally from the Central Valley. She moved to the Bay Area six years ago to go to law school. She finds dating in the Bay Area a bit of a challenge. "I heard a phrase once about finding men to date in the Silicon Valley, and I've come to think it is pretty true: 'The odds are good, but the goods are odd.'"

She has met a few guys here. "One really great one, and a few okay ones, and a few very inexperienced ones." Her last encounter was a mixed-bag. "The bad part about my last sexual experience was that he was very inexperienced. The good part was that because of his inexperience he was willing to try new things, eager to please and very appreciative. And he was decently big. (Of course size matters.)"

Recently, Jean was with "a guy four years younger than me. I met him at a bar and he called later that week. At the bar, I was pretty drunk and I ended up making out with him in front of my friends. The next week we went on a date and then went back to my house. He seemed pretty confident, making sexual comments and flirting all night. But when we got back to my house and ended up naked in my bed, I discovered he was very inexperienced. I kneeled down while he was standing up and gave him oral sex. He started saying things like "Oh my goodness gracious," and "How did you learn to do that?"

I almost laughed, except for that my mouth was full. I guess he'd never had a blowjob before. Even though he was inexperienced, I have to give him an 'A' for effort. He went down on me, even though I could tell he didn't know what he was doing, and he wanted to try many different positions. He was cute, but definitely too young and immature for me. I haven't spoken to him since he left my house the next morning."

Jean's most unusual encounter occurred back home in the Central Valley on the hood of her parents' car—while it was parked in their driveway. "I was a senior in high school, and at that age, in that town, there weren't a lot of places that you could go to have sex. One night, my boyfriend and I discovered that having me sit on the hood of my mom's new Cadillac was the perfect height with him standing. It was dark, but if someone would have driven by they could have seen us. I think the idea that we could be seen made it more exciting."

Jean's best encounter ever occurred a few months after breaking up with her boyfriend of nine years. "I met a tall, gorgeous guy at a bar and we ended up back at my house. He had such a great six pack, he barely had a belly button. And he was so huge that I was almost afraid of it. I was nervous about being with someone new after so long, but he made me feel very comfortable. He went down on me for so long I thought I was going to die, and at one point while he was down there, I offered to have him stop so that I could reciprocate, and he said not yet, and kept going. He was very talented in that department and in every other one as well. God was he beautiful. We ended up going on one date after that, and he wasn't that intelligent, so I didn't want to date him, but I was very tempted to keep him around and use him for sex. I didn't though."

Her ideal sexual encounter would be "with a guy who is big, knows how to please a woman and who can last a long time."

Naomi

Naomi, 21, is originally from Boston. She headed out west to "work in a faster-paced industry." She is an Economist and is currently single.

She's found the Bay Area dating scene much more friendly than back East. "Lot's of guys, and younger women are open minded and bi-curious. Also, most white guys here are open to dating an Asian-American woman, but back East some of the best guys (marriage material!) would only go with white girls," says Naomi.

Unfortunately, the quality of sex partners leaves something to be desired. "In other areas, I usually went with older, experienced men. Here I am mostly with younger guys, who are vigorous, but whose technique is not as refined as my more mature partners.

I meet guys in the gym, so they're really in shape. But they're too conservative in what they are comfortable doing. The watch porn and fantasize about doing things, but they're too reserved to actually perform their fantasies when I give them the chance."

Naomi's adventuresome nature led her online where she discovered an old flame. "I was with somebody I already had real sex with. He was a student in a class I was a TA for, we were re-living old times." She's also hooked up with someone she met on an alumni mailing list online.

Currently, Naomi is not interested in a relationship. Her last encounter was with a "guy that understood I wasn't looking for a committed relationship, but just wanted to be friends as I offered myself to him. I just invited him over to watch a Formula One race, and we relaxed in the hot tub afterwards, where I climbed on top of him and teased him to attention. I think the neighbors could tell what we were doing (I was topless), but I'm just house sitting, so that's not my problem."

One of her most unusual encounters occurred on an Amtrak train from Santa Clara to Berkeley. "Four of us, co-workers, none of us in relationships (with each other), were going home early after a long lunch to celebrate completing a project at work. We were talking about how even though we're professionals with good jobs, we still have roommates, but the roommate relationship is different from when we were in college.

We were talking about when we hooked up and brought somebody back to our room, we would have to be so quiet, or in some cases, room-mates would just brazenly have noisy (!) sex while we were in room. We were talking about how to do it quietly, and one of my coworkers reached in my skirt and started fingering me, daring me not to squeal or moan. I sat there looking across the table at the other couple, with them fully aware of what we were doing."

Barry

Barry is a 28 year-old Silicon Valley native. He works as a Data Networks Account Executive and describes himself as "single and swinging."

He's had five dates in the past month, and his last sexual experience was a rewarding one-night stand.

Barry offers the following rundown on the Silicon Valley dating scene: "The reason men here find it difficult to get dates is that most of the men are engineers. Lacking social skills, and good hygiene, they are shot down even on the rare occasion they get the guts up to make a decent pass at a woman.

On the other hand, sales and marketing professionals have way fewer problems, due to their outgoing nature and clean cut good lucks. They end up finding and going out with the beautiful women."

Paul

Like Barry, Paul chalks up the problems of Silicon Valley dating to the large number of engineers. Paul is a 33 year-old angel investor who lives in San Francisco.

"In San Jose, the heart of Silicon Valley, there are many engineers and few women. The ratio down there favors women. The scene is better up here in San Francisco. A lot of gay men means less competition for us straight guys in getting the good women. I'm glad I don't live in San Jose!" says Paul.

Paul finds it relatively easy to meet women, however "I am always looking for quality over quantity," says Paul, "and I have not yet found the right woman for a long-term committed relationship."

Paul moved to the Bay Area from the Midwest for "job opportunities, the lifestyle and the weather."

When asked if he's tried cybersex, Paul commented: "What the #&! is cybersex? Some things will always be better in person!"

Paul describes his last sexual encounter as somewhat unexpected. "My dating partner (not really girlfriend) wanted to go to bed alone so she could get up early for a big athletic event. Our kiss good night progressed and one thing led to another. Suddenly, my pants are down, her undies are around her ankles, and I'm sliding in and out of her. Unexpected sex like that is always a very nice surprise."

The most unusual place Paul's had sex was "my girlfriend's parents' kitchen floor. I was visiting my girlfriend at the time for the holidays. We had gone out for the evening, and come back to her parents' house late at night. We were sleeping in separate bedrooms and decided we had been 'good' long enough. We start going at it, right there against the kitchen table, knowing that we could have been caught by her parents at any moment. Imagine her Mom or Dad coming down for a glass of warm milk and finding me banging their daughter right there in their kitchen!"

Paul's best sex ever was with a nurse who made clever use of props. "I've dated a handful of 'over the top' erogenous, erotic women. The one who stands out in my mind is a nurse, who was a divorced mother of three. She took me into her bedroom, got out the stethoscope, took my pulse, and stripped me naked. We made love, and then she took my pulse a second time with the stethoscope. What do you know—my pulse was much faster after a good orgasm!"

Sally

Sally is a 28 year old pharmaceutical sales rep, originally from Redding, California. She moved here six years ago after her boyfriend from Chico State got a job in San Francisco. "I followed him down here, but after a while things didn't work out anymore," says Sally.

When asked how finding dates here compares to other areas, Sally comments: "It's easy to get dates, but hard to find men that aren't commitment-phobes. Also, I live in the Marina and all the men down here are looking for rich women with skinny bodies and big (oftentimes fake) boobs."

Sally is currently in a committed relationship, and has enjoyed sex more than ten times in the past month. While her sex life here is plentiful, Sally thinks wistfully back to her college days: "Nothing will compare to Chico State experiences."

Many of Sally's best sexual experiences have taken place on or near boats. Her most recent experience was on a houseboat full of people. "We were on a houseboat trip with 42 other people, and we sneaked a quickie in our room. We could hear at least a dozen people outside our window, but all we cared about was the heat going on in our room. We were so into it! The rocking of the boat didn't hurt either!"

Sally also enjoyed a nice rendezvous with a Navy boy, in her aunt's boathouse on Shasta Lake. "A nice Navy diver boy was up visiting my cousin, and the two of us really hit it off. After chatting for a while, it was pretty obvious we both were very into each other. I suggested we go for a walk, but I guess we both knew we were really looking for a place where we could explore each other's bodies in private.

The boathouse seemed like the perfect spot. My mom and aunt were hanging out by the water, right outside the boathouse. Fortunately, they didn't see us go in. We were alone!

We started kissing, touching and petting each other. We could hear the water lapping against the side of the boathouse. And, then, this nice Navy boy was lapping me! He slid my panties off my hips, and his head was between my legs, giving me the most incredible oral! It's amazing the things they learn in the Navy. That tongue!

I then knelt between his legs and returned the favor until he was rock hard, and we were both totally ready for penetration.

I was very relieved he had a condom with him, because at that point I wanted him between my legs so badly I was willing to throw all caution to the wind.

There was a couch in the boathouse, and I lay back with my legs spread, and he leaned over me, and thrust into me.

That Navy boy didn't just dive well under water! I was already so turned on, that the sensations were incredible.

We went at it, right there on the couch, fast and furious, with my mom and aunt still chatting away on the other side of the wall!

Years later, when I visit my aunt, I still get a warm glow every time I see that boathouse!"

Fran

Fran is a 27 year-old Data Modeler, who was born and raised in Silicon Valley. She is unmarried and currently in a casual relationship. Her sex life is plentiful, and when asked how many times she's had sex in the past month, Fran checked the "10+" box on her survey. Her last sexual encounter was with her dating partner and she rates it as an "eight." Fran elaborates: "It was with somebody that I've had sex with often enough to have a rhythm and road map already. It was sex in which we both knew what the other likes, but we were each new enough to each other not to be boring or predictable."

Fran's most unusual encounter happened last summer in the deep South. "I was working in Kodiak, AK for the summer," Fran says. "One of the boys I was sleeping with was mad at me and took off across a park. I ran after him, and when I caught up with him, we were in someone's backyard. I don't know whose yard it was, but we ended up having sex right then and there. He was not mad at me anymore after that."

Fran's best sexual encounter was a threesome. "A couple that I knew made it clear they wanted to have sex with me," Fran says. "So, one evening I stayed over and they both went down on me. It was incredible. We kissed and sucked and licked and squeezed all night. We finally fell asleep as dawn came. What a night!"

Natalie

Natalie is a 24 year-old consultant, who is currently unemployed. Natalie was born and raised in Silicon Valley. She is single, and prefers to meet people the old-fashioned way, rather than through online dating.

Natalie's had one date in the past month, which led to a sexual encounter. Natalie describes the sex: "The guy I had it with is someone I'm seeing on and off, and I think he's the hottest thing. But, it's always the same thing between us. He's a bit on the emotionally unavailable side. But, isn't that why we women love them? The sex itself… it was nice… very intimate because we are comfortable with our bodies regardless. It's always easy for us to pick things up where we left off."

The most unusual place Natalie's had sex is "at my workplace. Very fun. Basically, I had sex on the 36th floor of a San Francisco building, overlooking the Embarcadero."

When asked about her best sex ever, Natalie says: "Hmm… I usually am most aroused when signs of emotional intimacy precede physical intimacy. So, it's less the encounter than what comes before that makes it great sex."

Natalie's biggest dating disaster was with a dot-commer who thought he was King of the World. "I went out for drink with this guy who was so full of himself," says Natalie, "He was one of those 24 year olds who thought he was the smartest thing around. He started his own company and thinks it's the next big thing. Have some humility. And, he was talking to me as if was an old wise man with pearls of wisdom to share. Yuck!"

Natalie offers this final comment on the dating scene: "I hear that San Francisco has the best percentage of singletons out there. But, everyone complains they can't find anyone. Isn't that weird? Why is it so hard to meet people?"

Chapter Eight

So...what does it all mean?

When we started this project, we had few preconceptions. Friends and colleagues were eager to share their experiences, and it seemed there were few common threads. Some were enjoying fabulous sex lives, while others were pondering whether hymens could actually grow back if you were deprived of sex long enough.

We decided to take the survey online in order to reach a larger, broader audience. The results began pouring in within minutes of the site's launch. Everyone had a story to tell and a desire to tell it. The anonymity allowed respondents to be completely candid, and they were.

The survey was designed to elicit stories and provide data, from which we hoped we'd be able to spot a trend or two. Not being researchers, sociologists or scientists, we designed the survey to fit our needs. The data gathered is not scientific; we prefer to think of it as info-tainment. However, the responses were genuine and frank. Our respondents shared their humiliations and frustrations as well as their more titillating stories.

So after months of research, countless interviews and hundreds of surveys, what have we learned?

First, there is sex in Silicon Valley. And the so-called "geeks" in the valley are getting more than you'd think. As the Mecca of technology, Silicon Valley has always attracted large numbers of engineers and other techies. What's changed is the new appreciation women have found for these so-called "geeks." As one survey respondent from Boston said, "There are so many intelligent, creative 'engineer' types who apply the same type of inventiveness to sex. There are amazing men sitting behind computers thinking about sex all day—hot and ready to go!"

We also learned that the same spirit of innovation that has made the region a technological superpower is now being applied to the dating scene. And we learned that the transplants, who uprooted themselves from familiar surroundings and moved thousands of miles to settle in Silicon Valley, aren't afraid to charge ahead and try new things, like online dating and cybersex. The adventurous spirit that led them to the Valley leads them to rewarding sex lives, as well.

Most importantly, we learned that sex and love are powerful motivators. Whatever the obstacles and challenges, human beings will find a way to connect.

We hope these stories have entertained and inspired you.

About the Authors

"Kiana Tower" is actually two people. One of us is married, the other single. One is a transplant, the other a native of Silicon Valley. Both are in our early 30s, and we both work in the tech industry. *Sex in Silicon Valley* is our first book.

"Kiana Tower" is the fictional pen name we chose to use for this project. "Kiana" is a Hawaiian name, and Hawaii plays big into the origins of the book. And "Tower" is just a nice strong sounding name, and also a bit phallic, which fits along nicely with the fun we're having chatting about sex.

Why use pen names? Well, the authors of this book are professionals working at well-known Silicon Valley companies. To allow everyone to express themselves freely, we decided a pen name was the way to go.

We are real people, though. You can even contact us at kianatower@aol.com, and we will respond to your e-mail. Or take the sex survey at SexinSiliconValley.com and you may be featured in the sequel…

Cheers,
Kiana

Appendix

The Sex in Silicon Valley Survey & Results

SECTION I:

Age:

> *Average age: 30.6*
> *Men: 30.7*
> *Women: 29.2*

Gender:

> Male: *61%*
> Female: *39%*

Occupation:

> *Administrative: 6%*
> *Creative: 10%*
> *Engineer: 10%*
> *Executive: 7%*
> *Finance: 7%*
> *Professional (law & medical): 2%*
> *Sales/Marketing: 20%*
> *Student: 5%*
> *Tech (non-engineer): 13%*
> *Unemployed: 6%*
> *Other: 14%*

Are you originally from the Bay Area?

> Yes, I am a native: *38%*

No, I am a transplant: *62%*

If you are a transplant, where are you from?

What brought you out here?
  Career Opportunity: 45%
  Education: 10%
  Family: 8%
  Lifestyle: 25%
  Significant Other: 7%
  Other: 5%

How long have you lived in the Bay Area (non-natives)?
  Average: 4.7 years

Are you:
  Single: *77%*
  Married or Same-Sex Union: *10%*
  Separated: *3%*
  Divorced: *10%*

If you are single, are you (select the one which describes you best):
  Single and not in a relationship: *41%*
  Single and swinging: *22%*
  Single, in a casual relationship: *14%*
  Single, in a long-term, committed relationship: *17%*
  Single, co-habitating: *4%*
  Other: *2%*

How many dates have you had in the past month?
  Average, Men: *3.2*
  Average, Women: *3.2*

In general, how would you rate dating in Silicon Valley compared to other areas?

> More difficult to get dates: *47%*
> Easier to get dates: *25%*
> About the same as other areas: *18%*

How many times have you had sex in the past month?

> Average, Men: *4.5*
> Average, Women: *4.4*

In general, how would you rate the availability of sexual partners in Silicon Valley compared with other areas?

> Easier to find sex partners in SV: *36%*
> More difficult to find sex partners in SV: *36%*
> About the same as other areas: *22%*

In general, how would you rate your sexual experiences in Silicon Valley compared to other areas?

> Better: *29%*
> Worse: *26%*
> About the same as other areas: *34%*

In general, how would you rate the skill of your sexual partners in Silicon Valley compared to other areas?

> Better: *31%*
> Worse: *13%*
> About the same as other areas: *43%*

Have you ever had cyber-sex?

> Men: *55%*
> Women: *56%*

If you have had cyber-sex, did you ever meet your online sex partner in person?

>Men: *29%*
>Women: *27%*

Have you ever had sex with someone you met online?

>Men: *61%*
>Women: *38%*

When was the last time you had sex?

>In the past 24 hours: *25%*
>In the past week: *34%*
>In the past month: *15%*
>In the past six months: *10%*
>In the past year: *5%*
>What's sex?: *6%*
>No answer: *5%*

What best describes your last sexual partner?

>Significant other: *32%*
>Dating partner: *29%*
>Casual acquaintance: *11%*
>Friend: *9%*
>Co-worker: *3%*
>One-night stand: *13%*
>Yourself: *3%*

How would you rate your last sexual encounter on a scale of 1 to 10, with 10 being the highest?

>Men: *6.6*
>Women: *6.7*

SECTION II:

What was good or bad about your last sexual encounter?

What's the most unusual place you have ever had sex? Tell us the details…(please!)

Describe the best sexual encounter you have ever had.

Describe you biggest dating disaster.

Have a great true story you'd like to share? Tell us all about it!

Glossary

To protect the identities of our survey respondents, we allowed everyone to choose a pen name. Although, in retrospect, perhaps we should have been more specific in explaining the concept of a "pen name."

True to Silicon Valley style, most folks picked a "pen name" that came out sounding more like an AOL username. Since it's distracting to read a tale about someone named "MonkeyBoy" or "UrsaMajor" or "Mary Jane Naughty Bottom," we translated the more colorful names into normal sounding names. The names do not relate to the real names of our survey respondents. Since we intentionally set up our forms to be completely anonymous, we couldn't trace the real identities of our survey respondents even if we wanted to. (And we wouldn't want to, as that spoils all the fun of allowing people a forum to spill out their deepest darkest secrets and fantasies).

To make it easy for our survey respondents to find themselves in the book, here is a glossary of the pen names submitted with the surveys.

Barry McA = Barry: male, 28, data networks account executive
Bea = Betty: female, 30
belltop = Brett: male, 26, communications manager
BigBlonde = Barbara: female, 35, legal secretary
Carkeysmcgee = Cary: male, 23, unemployed
Chyna = Chyna: female, 25, audio/video producer
Cornelius = Cornelius: male, 24, finance
Curllup = Cathy: female, 20, student
Debbie = Debbie: female, 32, marketing manager
DizEdevL = Don: male, 28, "laid off"
Doug = Doug: male, 34
electricblue1980 = Elvis: male, 21
EZ = Ed: male, 41, social services

flicka = Faith: female, 33, designer
footgirl = Fran: female, 27, data modeler
Geldof = George: male, 33, sales & marketing
Gennifer Meatless = Jennifer: female, 30, marketing manager
gophigure = Gregory: male, 36, scientist
JamesBond = James: male, 28
Jean = Jean, female, 28, attorney
JF = Jack: male, 28
JoeJuice = Joe: male, 41, professional/business executive
Jon De La Luna = Jon: male, 32, lab technician
Kendra = Kendra: female, 36, project manager
Lina70 = Lisa: female, 31, systems analyst/unix systems administrator
LollyLikeALot = Laurie: female, 25, consultant
lthrlust = Luke: male, 39, manager
luckybastard = Lucky: male, 32, sales/marketing
M. Ridgewood = Max: male, 29, import/export business
Magdalene = Maggie: female, 48, student
Mary Jane Naughty Bottom = Mary Jane: female, 27, unemployed
MonkeyBoy = Michael: male, 34, web designer
Muffin = Mary: female, 27, content developer
Naomi = Naomi: female, 21, economist
Nicole = Nicole: female, 32, marketing consultant
notoriousangel = Natalie: female, 24, unemployed
pen name = Peter (yes, someone put down "pen name" as their pen name.): male, 27, student
PrivateInvestor = Paul: male, 33, angel investor
quattrogirl = Joy: female, 34, finance director
RandomCamel = Randy: male, 29, sales
Sally = Sally: female, 28, pharmaceutical sales rep
sdg001 = Sam: male, 31, human resources
Snow = Stan: male, 25, software engineer
steve-0 = Steve: male, 27, director of revenue management

Steve Y. = Stephen: male, works for e-commerce start-up
Suzie = Suzie: female, 34, graphic artist
tazgirl = Tammy: female, 26, counselor
TheRubenGal = Rory: female, 54, technical/applications/web designer
UrsaMajor = Marshall: male, 48, film maker
WG = William: male, 28, wine industry/sales
yachtslut = Yasmine, 32, female, n/a
Young & Bored = Bobby: male, 23, software engineer